Glasgow Boy's Walk of Life

Glasgow Boy's Walk of Life

Patrick Munro

Dedication

This is to all the people I've met, fought with, shared time with, shared a pint with and shared life with. God help them, it must have been difficult for themWhy does life have to be so complicated at times?

CHAPTER ONE

It all started when I was four years old in a flat in the East End of Glasgow, 1960. I remember waking up and my old grannie was there and an old guy with stains all down his shirt with no collar. He had a bunnet on in the house.

I got up and asked, "Where is my mammy?"

Grannie answered, "She's away tae get married."

I thought, *What is that?* But I continued bouncing up and down on the thin hard mattress, which was on a sofa bed in the living room, so there wasn't much up and down going on. I think that could have been the start of my rheumatic ankle problems and the hard skin on my heels.

I was a simple-minded wee guy, I think. Easily pleased at most. I started my first school just up the street. It was an old creepy-looking school with weird-looking people telling us all where to go. It was St Mark's.

In class, we got a tiny bottle of milk, which was kinda warm. Horrid stuff. The teacher was a woman, but she

1

had a beard, which really had me confused. As a four-and-a-half-year-old, that's a big thing to think out.

We got out for playtime mid-morning. I remember it being very sunny.

Two kids came up to me and said, "Are you new?"

"Aye," I said.

Boom. I got punched on the nose by one of them. They ran away laughing. I cried, but nobody helped me.

Back in class with a bloodied nose, the bearded one accused me of fighting and I got stuck in a corner. People have asked, how can you remember your first day at school?

Every time I'm in that area, I cringe…

Back in the house, I remember this guy who was there a lot. I got told his name was Da, but everyone called him Jim.

Then another guy was hanging about a fair bit, but not in the house. It was always dark when he was about. I remember my ma putting me in a big black pram. Yes, a pram. I was five years old and my feet were sticking out of it.

Anyway, I was told his name was Da too. Then this old guy who was always in the house used to scare me. He kept falling and walking into walls and the doors and everyone shouted at him. I was told to call him Da too. I later came to realise he was my granda, Hughie. He was almost blind and always pissed and smoked a stinking old pipe. He put a substance called thick black tobacco in it. Today, they would likely call it skunk, and it bloody stank.

He didn't get out much, as you can imagine, but whenever he did, who had to go with him? Yes, you guessed it. Me... I was his walking stick. He'd tell me which way to go, put his hand on my head, and being drunk, it was a heavy hand, hence my round shoulders, and off we'd go.

If it was a nice day, we would go to the shops. I learnt very fast where the shops were by his teaching, only to find out later that was his motive, so he could then just send me for his skunk and he didn't need to go out. Back then, a six-year-old could just go into a shop and buy tobacco. Think that's why I smoked at seven years old. Not the pipe though... I was nine and desperate for a puff when I had a go at that. First and last...

3

I think I was kinda happy with life then. We moved house to a ground floor flat, which I didn't like. The East End was full of really nasty people back then, really dark and creepy people, crooked and non-caring and would take anything you had. Nowadays, they are called politicians…

By the time I was about seven, I was gaining a few pals and neighbours knew me also, and word got about that I was a decent kid. So, I started to run for messages. For the posh people, that means running to local shops for groceries, fags, Irn-Bru, anything they needed and I got a wee tip for doing it. Sometimes the tip was, "run faster next time or I'll boot yer arse"…

We started finding ways to make a few bob, apart from the message run, which I had for me. We would go around knocking doors and asking for any empty ginger bottles and get money or sweets for them. We would get to know our streets very fast and watched who were the younger couples' flats as they were the ones who bought the Irn-Bru, so they would always have empties. If they told us to fuck off, we would go back later with a load of dog shite. There was always plenty of it at hand. We'd lay it outside their flat door, put newspaper over it, set it alight and bang on the door and run. They would open the door, panic when they saw the paper on fire and start stamping on it to put it out. You, by now, get the gist of the exercise.

Back to my night time da. It was a weird set up. His name was Pat. He was very nice. I barely remember him, but I remember getting pushed from Parkhead to Rutherglen, counting the night stars as I lay in my very cramped pram and watching my ma being very happy and smiling. She was a very good-looking lady, very slim and took pride in herself, especially going to see Da Pat.

We would arrive in this house with a big green hedge around a garden. I thought it was in the country, only to realise many years later it was the start of Toryglen. The house was always full of people. A lovely old woman I was told to call "Grannie McDunoch" used to put me on her knee. She looked like an orangutang in an apron. I always got a lot of attention and I loved it, especially from this wee woman called Auntie Rose, who had eyes that met in the middle and she had a lisp and a big thick shoe on one foot. To be honest, I was terrified of her, but she was very nice. When she spoke to me, she appeared to be looking at the wall. I was too young to realise it was her eyes. She couldn't focus on who she was talking to, and she would spray saliva when she spoke due to her lisp. So, most times, I was glad she was looking at the wall. They were like the Addams family, but they were funny and kind. This, I later was told, was my family, and "Da Pat" was my real da.

Back to Parkhead. I lived right next door to Celtic Park, which is now a car park. We got up to all sorts. Mainly trying to make money to survive. Turned out, "Da Jim" was the guy my ma married on the aforesaid day I was trying to bounce on my hard bed. He was a well-built, very young-looking guy, very quiet, never had much to say. All he did was sit on a chair watching TV and eating sweets by the bag full. His feet always were stinking. He was a butcher by trade, but hardly ever worked.

My wee ma always worked. She was in an oatcake factory by day in Rutherglen, then worked in the pubs at night. That was a tough call in those days. Pubs in the East End were very wild, but she handled it. She would get off the bus about 4, then rush home to get changed

6

and slap on the Max Factor make up and back out to work for 5:30 till closing at night, which was 10 then, which was strange because she never got home till 3 or 4 in the morning, but I'll save that for later…

After a short time, Da Pat disappeared off the scene, but I was still taken in the pram to see Grannie Orang-utang and the mob, until my legs hung out the pram too far not to be noticed. So, it was goodbye family number one. As my ma never had the time or money to take me by bus, I was never allowed to mention my "other family" visits to Grannie Sophie, Granda Hughie or number two da, Jim. It was me and my ma's secret, which I kept all my life.

CHAPTER TWO

One cold night, me and a pal called Ikey were skint and hungry and bored. I was about nine years old.

Ikey was very poor and in Parkhead in the sixties, very poor was like living in a makeshift shed in India. His ma and da were both alcoholics. His da, old Wullie, was always pissed. He would stand at his close entrance and challenge people to fight. Man or woman, or even the odd stray dog. He was a rough old guy with a bent nose and always wore an army belt of which Ikey and his poor old ma Sally would feel around their heads and backs whenever it suited him. Wullie was a violent old bastard, but karma always beckons.

Two closes down from Ikey, a gypsy family moved in. Now the mother, Mary the Tinker, was as hard as nails and drank like a fish too and liked a fight. She drank and made a reputation in the local beer house called Flynn's. She was in many a fight on a Friday night. As kids, we would go and wait for them coming out and we would watch them all fighting. Mary the Tinker was mostly involved. Old Wullie never went out to pubs, mainly because he was always drunk and would get run over by a bus, so he drank indoors.

Now, the gypsy woman heard about me as the shop runner and summoned me to go get her fags, even though the shop was fifty yards away. She was okay with me always and gave me a shilling for myself. To be honest, she scared me shitless, so I was always extra nice through fear. I remember going into her house and her wee husband was sitting on the chair with his bunnet and scarf on. I never saw the poor guy again ever...

She had a dog who had wandered away. She was out looking for it and me and Ikey and another guy helped her. There was a bit of noise created by us shouting the dog's name. Back then, dogs were straying all over the place and every fucking dog was called Shep or Blackie. Nightmare

Old Wullie, on hearing the noise, came outside and started shouting and bawling as usual, but Mary the Tinker was not in a good mood. They had a few words and next thing, Wullie had a swing at her. He got her on the side of the face. She came back at him with the chain dog lead she was holding and swung it right over his head. His forehead opened up like a pomegranate. He went down and she went mental on him, kicking into him, putting the head on him when he was down. She fought like an animal.

Ikey was shouting, "Do the old bastard, Mary. Do him."

All the beatings Ikey took were raging out of him.

I thought Wullie was dead. He was just about. He never was himself after that and died about a year later. Even the cops came team handed to arrest Mary. A regular occurrence.

I later bought a pup from her for 10p, Rikky. He lived for fifteen years.

Mary the Tinker moved away. Never seen her again or her wee man or the dog who wandered and caused the fight.

Getting back to the cold night we were hungry and bored. Barr's factory was in the East End next to St Michael's School. There was a covering of snow the night

11

we decided to scale the wall which took us onto Barr's roof. It looked down onto the trucks in the loading bay, which were loaded and ready to go for the next day. Ikey, being very skinny, dreeped down onto the trucks. It was dark, but the snow on the ground gave us light.

He got under the canvas cover on a truck and started throwing up bottles of ginger. Now, back then, we really only had Irn-Bru, cola and orange. Nothing fancy.

Ikey started throwing up bottles. I caught them and threw them down on the snowy grass. After a bit, the night watchman heard us. He shouted and had his dog. We bolted and bagged our blag. We bolted to a wee shed we had behind the black horrible tenements. We lit our candle and, low and behold, the bottles were a different colour to what we knew. It turned out Barr's were releasing new flavours to the shops the next day and we picked the truck that had them. Pineapple, red kola, limeade and ginger beer. We struck gold. We drank the lot and kept the bottles to show our pals the next day. Well, we couldn't take them for a refund…

I had another pal called Ronnie. Now, he was interesting to the point that one day he was my best mate and the next he was like my nemesis. He was always the alpha male. Strong, popular, always had a good supper on the table, which was rare for any of us. His wee da, Pat, was a bricky (he helped build houses) and made decent money.

Ronnie had four sisters and two brothers. His sisters were real nice girls, always very good to me. His eldest brother Jim was a cracking guy. Also, the other one, Anthony, was weird. Always thought he was Steve McQueen until he got put into prison for six months. When he got out, he became Steve McQueer. In the nick, he took it up the boys' gate and liked it. And that's the way he stayed for as long as I can remember.

I was around his family very much, if only at times to get a decent feed. My two favourites were Jim the eldest, and Margaret, second eldest sister. Both of them had their young lives taken before they were twenty-one. Jim got drunk and was a victim of a hit and run driver, and Margaret got drunk and choked on her vomit. Their poor ma Alice never got over it and became a desperate alcoholic. Wee Pat, the da, ended up the same. The youngest of the family, Maureen, married some mad guy while he was in Carstairs Prison. She had four kids then became an alcoholic also and got the four kids taken from her. A whole family destroyed mainly through alcohol one way or another, but "always spoilt" alpha Ronnie survived, as expected.

It turned out he was very jealous of me. I was a very good-looking kid. He wasn't. I was liked by the girls. He wasn't. But, he got great toys and stuff at Christmas. I didn't. He was always well fed. I wasn't. We played football for the school team. He got player of the year. I was always a sub.

He got everything. I got fuck all. But I tasted Barr's pineapple with Ikey before he did, and he couldn't handle that. He hated poor Ikey too… Idiot. I stayed in contact with him until we were about twenty, then we just went our own ways. No great loss, but I did miss his brother and sister. More than he did, I think.

CHAPTER THREE

Between the ages of about eight to thirteen were not great years for me as I remember we were so poor. My ma and Da Jim churned out two kids by the time I was eight and another three by the time I was twelve. He would work, then wouldn't work. This went on throughout.

We had nothing, but I kept running messages now my tips were going to feed everyone in my family. It was porridge before school and porridge for supper after school. Sometimes without milk.

When Da Jim did work, he gambled heavy on the horses and mostly lost everything.

I remember three different times our electricity was cut off because the bill wasn't paid. Two of those times were at Christmas/New Year. I remember a neighbour, wee Mrs McMillan, brought us in some bananas on Christmas morning and a loaf of bread. That, thankfully, was our

Christmas dinner that year. Well, at least it was different I was told.

Mrs McMillan, our next-door neighbour, was a lovely wee soul. Drank cheap sherry seven days a week, always pissed. In the summer, her and my ma would sit outside in her garden. We had a strange neighbour who lived two floors above on the top floor, Mr Simpson, who had a massive plastic ear. Horrible-looking thing. And he had no hair. Story was his lug got blew off in the war and, like a glass eye, he could remove it from its fixing.

One day, when Ma and wee Mrs Mac and the kids were all in the garden, Mr Simpson came to his window, lowered his plastic ear down tied to a long piece of string and shouted, "Hey, I'm listening to yous."

Well, they all screamed and ran like a bat out of hell. He was pissing himself laughing, hanging over the top floor window. Then his false teeth fell out and hit wee Mrs Mac right on the head. Scary, but hilarious when I think of it… I wonder if he ever found a wife?

Old Grannie passed away not long after my ma got married to Da Jim. I was five years old. My ma was the youngest of seven sisters and she looked after old Grannie and Granda full time. Don't think Da Jim would have been any good.

Old Granda Hughie died when I was nine. He was sixty-four, but from a nine-year-old's eyes, he looked like ninety.

There was a wake set up, and all these aunties and uncles and cousins arrived. Usually, it was for a free swally at these things I later learnt. Anyway, the house was packed. Women wore black, men wore black suits and white shirts and black ties. Windows had white blinds, or white bed sheets, covering them for ten days. The scene was set for a party.

Old Hughie was lying in a bed in the bedroom, dead. I had a quick look at him and thought he was asleep drunk, as was regular.

Now I had a couple of aunties. Well, a few. One of my ma's sisters, Jean, was mental. She feared nobody, fought everybody who looked at her, and she was a heavy drinker. She even took on Mary the Tinker and beat her

17

up in the pub. Auntie Jean was a violent, very feared woman. She was always around us to protect us as my ma was a very gentle woman who hated violence.

Her sister Betty, who came up from Liverpool, had arrived and her and Jean hated each other. I had never met Betty, so I never knew much about her. I learnt very quick that night.

Once the wake was in swing, everyone having the bevvy, mostly whisky and beer, Jean and Betty stayed apart and never spoke, so the deal was each of the sisters were to take a turn and go and sit with old "dead" Hughie and have their peaceful words to him before he donned the wooden house coat.

It was going okay till Auntie Jean went in. Within ten minutes, all hell broke loose. She was pissed out of her head and screaming, "He's no dead. My da's no dead. He moved. He's no going into a coffin!"

Well, that was it. Utter panic started. I remember he'd been dead for three days at this point and the room smelt like a back street butcher shop. Betty ran in with the men trying to hold her back, but it was no good. She got to Jean, fighting and pulling hair, biting, punching, kicking.

I was at a distance watching it. They fell onto the bed on top of Hughie laying into each other.

My ma was shouting, "For God's sake, yer gonny hurt my da."

It was like a saloon fight. Then the men got fighting and Betty got dragged away. The bedroom door was off the hinges, the bed covers on old Hughie got dragged off a bit and one of his old rotten feet was showing. It was kinda blue, so was his face by this time. Thank God they got him flat packed the next morning...

The funeral went ahead. It was October 19th. I don't know where the money came from and after it, most people went their own ways.

Auntie Betty came back with my ma. I went out with my pals to play football.

Getting hungry later on, I went to my house and my ma, Weird Da Jim and Auntie Betty were all in the living room. Auntie Betty had a few scratches on her face from the battle with Auntie Jean.

Ma said, "Jim, you're going home with Auntie Betty for a wee while to Liverpool."

I asked all in one breath, "Where's Liverpool? What about school? What about my pals? When am I coming back? I don't even fucking know her."

"Never mind all that. You're going and you're going back with her tonight."

Later that night, I was on an old rickety bus on the way to Liverpool. It was dark and I couldn't see anything outside. Auntie Betty spent most of the time talking to the driver as we were right behind him. All I thought about was her strange accent and was worried I was going to talk like that when I came back.

Back then, it took about nine hours to get to Liverpool and I discovered I wasn't a good traveller on a bus. I spewed till there was nothing left inside me, and most of it went over the driver's coat which was being used to keep me warm from the cold draughts coming in the doors. It was the worst journey of my whole life in many different ways.

We arrived in the city of *The Likely Lads* as daylight was breaking. I felt ill, it was very cold and I felt completely lost.

We then waited ages for another bus and later arrived at her house to be met by a large dog barking in her kitchen.

My ma had all these sisters. The oldest had fourteen kids. Biggest family in Glasgow at the time. They all got their photo on centre pages in The Citizen newspaper. They looked like the Broons and the Bash Street Kids all in one.

Another, Sadie, had eleven kids. Another had eight. I ended up in Kirby, Liverpool with an auntie I didn't know, and she had thirteen kids. They all got out of bed one after the other to look at me. I felt like Oliver Twist.

When I left Glasgow the night before, I had a ma, a da I hardly knew who didn't give me any attention, a da who was my own but had vanished into the darkness, and a brother aged four and a sister aged one. And a dog whose name appeared to be "Fuck Off" as that's all everyone ever said to it. And now this. I was so confused and alone, in amongst thirteen kids and an aunt I knew nothing about. All of who I was told were "my family". I cried for a few days and nights.

After about a week, I settled down a bit. The younger kids were more curious about my accent rather than me. I need to say Auntie Betty was very protective of me to start. A couple of the kids were a bit nasty to me. I was another mouth to feed in a family who had nothing and fought to survive. She had no husband. If she heard anyone slagging me, they would get a slap and a stern word from her. Story ended.

She had a middle son Jack, who was aged fourteen, five years older than me. He liked me and took me under his wing, took me to the den and to meet a few of his pals. They were all great guys. Pure Scousers from a rough end of town. That was when I started to like Kirby. Before I knew it, I was smoking fags, drinking beer, stealing, skipping into the local picture house and the swimming. They hardly paid for anything. My world arrived...

CHAPTER FOUR

After about ten weeks, not long before Christmas, I got the calling via a letter from my ma. It was time to come home.

"No chance," I said, but my school was on to her to get me back.

Also in the letter was, "I've got a lovely surprise for you…"

I learnt a lot later in life that when ma says, "I've got a surprise for you", it was time to worry.

Now I was crying again because I had to come back. I was nine and a half at this point. I was put on a bus to sit with the conductor on the front double seat and make the long tedious journey back. I was to be met on arrival in Glasgow. Today, that wouldn't be allowed.

Back in Glasgow, I was met by a big cousin who used to stay with us a lot. One of the Bash Street Kids. Every time she got tossed out, she would stay with us. I remember it was snowing and very cold that morning in Glasgow, but Auntie Betty and Cousin Jack made sure I had warm clothes and plenty of sandwiches for my journey. Salmon spread on dry bread. Pure luxury. And I scoffed the lot, even though I was sick on the return trip. That was the last time I saw Jack and Auntie Betty. Jack died last year aged sixty-five. He took two strokes and was an alcoholic. Lovely guy he was. I'll never forget him.

I arrived back in Parkhead excited at seeing my ma and my "surprise". I went into the living room and Weird Da Jim was watching TV.

"Where's Ma?" I shouted.

"She's in bed," he answered.

I jumped into her room and Ma was in bed. The electric fire and bed lamp were on. Curtains shut.

"Ye awrite, Ma? I'm home, I'm hungry."

She said, "Say hello to yer wee brother."

Then I noticed a wee white shawl and a baby in it in her arms.

"Who's this?" I asked.

"It's yer new wee brother Walter. This is the surprise I told you about."

I looked at my cousin. She said she was not to tell me.

Weird Da Jim was in the living room not giving a shit as usual. The other two kids were hanging about the house. The house felt strangely quiet being used to the mad but funny house I left behind.

"Can I have my dinner? I'm hungry."

"There's nothing for dinner. Yer da is no working. You need to go upstairs to Jeanie and ask her if she can lend yer ma something."

I realised I was back home.

Jeanie also had a man who never worked and four kids to feed. They were as poor as us, but they were the first to pass down a live cable to our house when the power was cut, until they got caught.

Weird Da Jim was never bothered with me after old Granda Hughie died. I wasn't his kid, and he knew my real da, Pat, lived not far away. Well, he did for a wee while. Da Jim had a mother, four sisters and a brother. Three of the sisters hated me. His eldest was nice, as was his elder brother.

I remember when I was five or six, I was sitting on a stool on a very rare visit to his mum's and his sister spat

25

on me and called me a bastard. She was about fourteen. I can still remember the school uniform she had on. He did nothing to protect me. I could have told Auntie Jean but I knew what she would have done to her, so I let it go. But I hated her and her two sisters, because they hated me, and his old bag of a mother who I was forced to call Nana. I'll add to that later…

Christmas passed as usual, and wee Walter was never very well, always sick and crying. I remember the nurse who always came in a dark green uniform and a wide hat on. Then he was in hospital.

I turned ten and was taking a part in helping my ma with wee Walter, but even as a ten-year-old I could sense something wasn't right. One morning in September, I was woken up by Ma's screams. I jumped up, dived into the living room and saw Weird Da Jim pinning my ma against the wall.

I shouted, "Hey, you, fucking leave her alone."

She wasn't making sense. Just then I looked in Walter's pram and he was dead. His eyes wide open, very pale, and brown fluid at the side of his mouth. His wee dummy was beside his mouth, stained brown also. Now I was oblivious to Ma's screams and I was focused on my wee brother lying dead. He was nine months. Tragic. But he was out of the pain he must have been in to be crying the way he did. Rest his wee soul.

His wee white coffin was carried out to a hearse and a funeral was practised. I think me and him would have got on. I felt a bond with him. Maybe because I helped my ma to nurse him, clean sick from him and change his nappies. He was the only one. He would have been about fifty now.

CHAPTER FIVE

I was back at school and trying to get on with life. I was on the school football team and I was doing great at school. I was working hard to get to St Mungo's All Boys School in Townhead. To earn that privilege, I had to be in the top three in our primary school. Two of the guys in my class were very clever and had kinda well-off parents. But I had been advanced six months in my year, so I was clever too.

We did our exams and I made third place behind Sherlock and Dr Watson. I qualified for St Mungo's senior secondary. Now this was a major achievement for me in my young life, but it didn't last long. As bloody usual...

I was very proud of myself by qualifying, but I had the old green eye from my so-called pal. But that wasn't my concern. Knowing what lay ahead, I was very worried about possible embarrassment... Well, not possible, certain.

When you qualify for a school like St Mungo's, it's like today's version of Jordanhill in the west of Glasgow: public school for the public elite. And what comes with that is the requirement of full uniform and accessories, like gym kit and the like. Then two buses were required to get me there. That meant money. What chance had I got? We had none of what was needed.

Sherlock and Dr Watson kept ribbing me about this, knowing I had shit all and laughing at me saying I would get thrown out the first week. I wouldn't give in.

I went to my ma and said, "Look, Ma. I can find second-hand uniform."

I knew it hurt her, but she had nothing. She borrowed money and took me down to the Briggait flea market. I got used grey trousers, ripped at the seam, one used shirt, plastic brown shoes, and a heavy woollen man's sized cardigan. Winter was coming, so I needed to be warm. She knew what was coming. I didn't at the time.

The day came. I was all excited and didn't care that I never had the uniform, and I had bus fare too. I had to get a bus from Parkhead to Trongate, then a bus from

Trongate up the high street to Townhead. Took about an hour all in.

That morning, I was all togged and proud that I never noticed how cold it was outside till I was outside. Raining and frozen. By the time I got to school, I was soaked and the heavy woollen cardigan weighed a ton, and by now it was down to my knees. But it covered the saddle stiches my ma made sowing the side of my second-hand trousers, so that was a plus.

I arrived. The school was creepy like St Mark's. It had big massive gates and all the first- and second-year guys were waiting for the new starts. Teachers were Marist Brothers. They all wore long black gowns and looked like monsters. I was shitting myself and, by now, stood out as every one of them had full uniform on and I didn't.

There was a massive lake-like puddle in the playground just near the shed. Next thing, I got grabbed by a bunch of them swinging me arms and legs to throw me in. All of a sudden, I got let go and dropped to the wet ground and they all left. Puzzled but relieved, I got up, wrang out my cardigan and checked the saddle stitches on my

31

trousers, knowing when I got into class the cardi would have to come off.

This guy said, "Awrite? You're okay. They won't bother you."

I didn't know this guy, but he said we played football together. Then I remembered when I played for the school team at my primary school. I was subbed that morning. We were playing St Mungo's. Then their manager said to our manager he was a player down, so he stuck me in to play for them to make up the numbers. I didn't like this, so I played the best game of my life and kicked one off the line to stop my school from scoring. I wasn't popular for that, but I made sure they wouldn't do that again. Well, they never did it again. I got kicked out of the school team that weekend.

This guy who saved me from drowning remembered me as he was in that St Mungo's team. Great memory he must have had. He even remembered my name.

He said, "Don't worry, Jim. I'll make sure you're okay."

Brilliant, I thought.

His elder brother was at the school too, so I was sorted. Or so I thought.

On my second week, we were going to gym and told to bring gym kit, which was a white T-shirt with a blue band on the neck rim, navy shorts and black sandshoes. Our parents were told this before we came and how important it was, but that letter must have lit the coal fire. *What was I going to do?* I thought. Remember, I wasn't even eleven yet...

Back then, "Dylon dye" was popular. I found an off-white old T-shirt in a drawer. I sat and picked at the neck stitching till it came away, dyed it in a basin with navy dye, dried it at the fire and restitched it back on with white thread. All on my own. I remind you, readers, I was almost eleven years old. I then found old football shorts and dyed them also. I bought the dye from my paper run money.

On gym day, the pressure was off me as I had my kit and I travelled to school happy that morning.

We were in the changing room and I put on the kit. Everyone was laughing at me. The neck rim had started to fall off as I didn't sew it right and it looked like shit. My shorts were all patchy as I never done them right. The P.E. teacher called us all out and I was shitting it again.

33

Happiness never lasts long. He took one look at me, gave me a slagging and made me sit on the bench. No sympathy or empathy, just a total arse he was. It was the start of my thinking, *I shouldn't be here...*

CHAPTER SIX

Back at the house, Weird Da Jim had found a job.

Great, I thought, *because winter is biting in and I'm starting to only get bus fare to Trongate, which means I've a half-hour walk up the high street.* When you're ten and a half, on a cold wet wintry day, it's a task and having never had any breakfast at times, I was tired and weak. I always remember the horrible smell when I got off the bus at Trongate. There was the Whisky Bond not far away and Tennent's Brewery to the east. Depending on the wind, you got the waff of the hops. Awful…

My best memory of my time at St Mungo's was one day when I had a few bob I got from the previous day running a few shop runs. It was a Thursday, so rather than spend it that day, I kept it for the Friday as back then chip shops only opened at lunch time on a Friday and at lunch break everyone bolted to the chippy.

I had never done this previously because I never had any money, but I made sure that on this Friday I would be there with the rest of them.

I was in the queue and could smell the vinegar and hear the big fryers and the sizzle of the chips. I heard the sound I wanted to hear: "Who's next?"

I shouted, "A bag a chips, plenty salt 'n' vinegar and broon sauce and a thick roll."

Now here was the good part. You asked the woman to half the roll, take away the inside dough and soak the two halves with vinegar.

The wee woman was very patient as she knew what we wanted.

I went outside and sat on the wall of the old St Mungo's church. I was starving. I opened the chips, got the two halves of the roll (it was like a baguette) and packed the chips covered in salt, vinegar and sauce into the vinegar-soaked walls of the roll. I did that to the two halves, looked at it for a second and got my gnashers right into it. Sauce and vinegar squeezed out of every opening, including the sides of my mouth. It was all coming through my wee fingers. If you've never tried it, you should. It's heaven. Do the first one, then do the second. Same sensation on both counts.

I was bursting at the seams of my tiny undernourished wee frame. At that point, nothing mattered The gym outfit, the long cardigan, the burst trousers, the plastic shoes, who my da was, who my brother and sister were and, of course, all the shit I was taking from others in school. For ten minutes, I didn't have a care in the world. I'll never forget that feeling for as long as I live...

A couple of weeks passed. I knew a few guys at school, but I wasn't one of the lads. I was getting by, but I wasn't doing well in class. By now, I wasn't liking this school and I was being picked on by a couple of teachers. Mainly because I was too tired to walk. I was the worst dressed in the class or school.

A teacher called Murphy pulled me out of the line up on a very cold morning because someone at the back of the line lobbed a snowball at him and hit him on the nut. He pulled me because, to gain friendship, I became a clown and did stupid things, just to try to be popular and get some of the others off my back. He knew this. When we got to class, he took me right away while my hands were cold and gave me six rapid hits of the belt. For those lucky ones who have never had the belt, it was fucking painful, especially if it got you on the soft skin on the wrist part. And especially if your wee hands were cold.

Another teacher was a tall skinny creepy guy we called Cecil. He looked like the actor Cecil Parker, hence the nickname. He was evil, and looked evil, and spoke very silently. His teeth were rotten and he wore old small round-framed glasses. A perfect paedo type. He taught French. I was scared of him and always kept my distance. He kept the belt in a long pocket in his creepy long black cloak so that it didn't bend.

Another badass was a wee maths teacher called Dada Kelly. Wee proper bastard. Ex-army and hated everyone over four feet eight inches because he was four feet seven inches. He hated everyone under that because he felt powerful over them.

By now, I'd had enough. I was making plans to get out of there and join my pals in the local school for morons, but they were happy morons. Well, they never knew any better.

I came home one day and Weird Da Jim was in, which was unusual as he was supposed to be at work. So, I thought, *Here we go again. No use asking what's for dinner...*

"Where's my ma?" I asked. I was hoping for the same reply my grannie gave me the first time I asked the same question: "Away tae get married."

But no, it wasn't, so I was stuck with this guy who, after six years, I still only knew his name was Jim and he ate lots of sweets.

"She's no here," he said, "She's in hospital."

"What's wrong?" I asked.

"Never mind," he said.

I thought, *Well, at least we're having a conversation at last.*

That night, I still didn't know where my ma was.

I asked again, "Where is my ma? I want tae go see her in hospital."

39

"No, you have tae watch the weans while I go tae hospital."

He came home later and said, "You're no gain tae school tomorrow."

Great, I thought. It was snowing and frozen. *Yes, a long lie in bed.*

I said, "Okay, am I going tae watch my brother and sister?"

"No, you're going to stay with Auntie Georgie."

Who the fuck is Auntie Georgie? I thought.

"Who's she?" I said.

"Never mind. You'll find out tomorrow. You and your brother are going to stay with her for a while."

Now I was pissed off and upset and crying, worried about where my ma was.

"Where does she live? What about school?" School was of no concern at all to me, but I had to play it out.

"You're no going to school. Nae money for that."

So, next morning, it was pissing down sleet and snow and we all left for the bus to sweet Auntie Georgie's house. Wherever it was.

Weird Da Jim was carrying my sister who was about one year old. I'd got my brother's hand who was about six years old. I was eleven. What lay ahead for us?

I was planning my escape from St Mungo's. I'd had enough of the humiliation, the bullying from teachers and me acting like an idiot to gain friendship from guys I didn't know, or didn't care about me. My plan was to come home late and say to my ma that I was always sick on the bus and had to get off and walk it, which then resulted in me being late and falling behind on my lessons.

The reason for this idea was because she got a letter from school a week before. We had a maths exam and I was just so pissed off with wee Dada Kelly I thought, *Fuck him*. He handed out exam papers and gave us so much time to do it. While everyone was giving it their best, I sat drawing on the exam paper.

Time up. He picked on a wee guy to collect the papers, which we were told to leave on our desks face down. I

41

was sitting back watching the response. He was reading the papers one by one, not marking them at this point.

All of a sudden, he paused. I could see his rotten wee red face getting redder. He looked around and immediately ran up and grabbed me by the neck and dragged me out. He was at his desk and he had me in a half nelson hold. I could smell his rotten gown. Minging.

He was squeezing my neck and shouting, bearing in mind I was a bit bigger than him by now, "What the devil is this, boy?" three or four times.

Well, I was thinking while foaming at the mouth, *let your fucking grip go and I'll try and speak.* He threw me over his desk, and I thought, *He's gonny do me up the arse. Please not in front of the class.* It was bad enough having to wear the cardigan, which after two months of winter rain looked like a woollen coat, and the plastic sandals which by now had got holes above and below and looked like something Jesus wore kicking about the desert, or wherever he hung out with his pals.

He pulled out the belt and started whacking me all over the place.

"Hold your hands out," he shouted.

42

So, I stood and clasped my hands out, palms upwards.

One, two, three, four, he gave me. I was stinging. I could see the anger in him. On the fifth stroke raging down, just as it got to my hands, I pulled my hands apart and the belt came through them with force and he whacked himself right on his balls and thighs. He went to grab me and I punched him in the face. I was then dragged up to the headmaster and got another four whacks from him.

In hindsight, I think the headmaster didn't like him. He was a nice mild-spoken guy, and was a bit sympathetic with me, but I wanted to be expelled, but he didn't do it.

We were on the bus to this mysterious Auntie Georgie. I was half excited and half shitting myself. On arrival, she actually didn't stay as far as I had dreaded, but still a distance up the East End. Weird Da Jim appeared to know her well. She seemed pleasant enough, but her hubby was a bit strange. I remember him being tall, thin and just standing behind her. Obviously, she was the alpha…

"Right, Jim. Don't worry. They will be fine," she said.

He left. Never said goodbye, never introduced us to her, and left with my wee sister. Me and my wee brother were standing in the hallway. The house was spotless, not like ours, and it had stairs. I had never been in a house with stairs. There were a lot of doors.

The hubby went into the living room, sat on the chair and just kept looking at us through the half closed door. The woman lifted the bag which was on the floor (which I recognised as my ma's bag). It had our bits of clothes in it.

"Right, boys. Come upstairs to your bedroom."

We followed her up. I was still holding my brother's hand.

My brother and me had hardly spoke to each other by then. In fact, I hardly knew him. He was a very quiet wee guy, never cheeky like me. He just sat around the house playing with the odd broken toy. He wore weird spectacles, and I only knew his name.

We entered the bedroom. It was all bright and tidy. Everything had its place. It was about early afternoon.

She asked, "Have you two had lunch?"

44

My brother looked up at me in confusion.

"Err no. In fact, we haven't had supper from yesterday," I said.

"Oh dear. Come and get some lunch."

She made us soup and bread. I was chatty but my wee bro wasn't. He just sat and never ate.

I said, "Hey, you idiot, eat it. It may be all we'll get."

So, he nibbled away. I scoffed mine. Then the hubby came into the kitchen. Never spoke to us, but I was watching him now I had a brother to protect. So, I stared him out. He made a cup of tea and left to watch TV.

Me and my brother ate up our food and I wondered what was coming next. He didn't say much. Well, he never did. Always a quiet wee guy. But I could see he was uncomfortable. He didn't know them and he hardly knew me, but he knew who I was at least.

"It's getting late now" were the words I didn't want to hear from Georgie.

"Come, I'll show you your room."

Upstairs we went. I took hold of my brother's hand. They were cold and sweaty. He was scared, and so was I…

45

We were led into an upstairs room. It was bright and clean. Not like we had been used to. Our bed had doors on it. It was called a bed cabinet, like a mattress in a shed.

I quite looked forward to the experience. Only thing was the room was freezing.

"Right, boys, bath time."

Now I was shivering. Who was gonny bath us? Not fucking Herman Munster downstairs I hoped. And why were we getting a bath? I could not remember ever having a bath, to be honest, even though there was one in our house. It was usually for spiders racing each other to try to get out of it, like me and my brother were about to be doing.

It was still daylight and we were about to be stripped and bathed in front of each other. This Auntie Georgie was away to get a towel with me and my brother like two of Hitler's prisoners waiting to go into the cyanide showers. We looked as underfed as those poor buggers were.

She came up and said, "Right, boys, clothes off for bath."

Like hell I was. I wouldn't even do that for my ma. I was eleven years of age with the build of a five-year-old, and the winkle to match.

46

"No," I said, "I will sort us out, with the door shut."

She obliged. I was embarrassed too because our underwear wasn't like you saw on TV adverts all bright and white. More like the boxers Jesus had on when he was getting crucified, all baggy and filthy and only held up with a nail.

I was still watching for Herman to make an appearance from downstairs, but he didn't, so me and bro got washed with the door shut. I washed our pants in the bath, not thinking about how we were going to dry them. The bath water was kind of cold, so we washed up fast and tried to scramble out of the bath like the mad spiders did.

The house didn't have heating back then, usually paraffin heaters which were stinking but effective. But I didn't see or smell one, so I put my trousers and jumper back on my damp wee skinny body in a hurry shivering like a nervous hyena and got my bro dried and dressed. He too was cold and shivering.

I opened the door and shouted that we were finished. Both he and her came upstairs.

"What are you doing with your clothes on again? They need to be washed. They're filthy."

I could have replied, "It's okay, we sat in the bath with them on to wash them," but it wouldn't have worked.

"Where are your pyjamas?"

My brother looked up at me, confused.

"We don't have any," I retorted, now getting extremely embarrassed.

Bolt in the neck Herman looked at us with sympathy. "The kids need some extra clothes, Georgie. It's not their fault." And then he went back downstairs.

Now I was sorry about what I said about the guy. He seemed okay.

Well, the clothes needed washing, so away she went and brought a couple of shirts and told us to wear them, which we did. I assumed one was Herman's and one was hers going by the length difference, but they had been ironed and cleaned.

"Just wear these to bed till I can get you pyjamas."

They had this large house up East End which was surrounded by fields and an old school. Greenfield, it was called. Then I recognised the house Weird Da Jim had me at, his mother's house across the road, six years earlier. The time his sister spat on me. So, Georgie must have been a friend to them of some kind. Now I felt uncomfortable in case the ugly sisters paid a visit. If they did and she had anything to say to me, I would have defended myself this time. I would have spat back at the pig.

At my young age of eleven years, I was growing an attitude against people who were bad to me and I was always on my defensive side.

Me and bro were in our beds by 8 p.m., but to be honest we were very tired due to the day we had. My wee brother was not saying much. He was only five years old and I knew he was scared and relying on me. I was eleven and feeling so lost and lonely and wondered what lay ahead. I put bro in against the wall. I was on the outside, so I would know if he got up for any reason.

We fell asleep pretty fast as I remember, even though the room was very cold, we had each other's body heat.

I woke up and it was light. I didn't feel right. It was freezing. Then I felt wet. My bro was awake and I realised he'd peed himself during the night.

49

I got up, got our wet shirts off and took the sheet off the bed. We were both shivering. I didn't know what to do. The bed was very wet and I didn't want him getting into trouble. He was too young to be embarrassed, but I wasn't. I looked outside to see if there was a back court to hang the sheet out. The windows were all wet and water was on the windowsills.

Fuck, I thought. *Has he been pissing on the windows too?* But it was condensation, as most houses had back then, due to not opening the windows due to lack of coal and money.

He started crying.

"Don't worry," I said, "It's okay."

But he wanted our ma and his da, Weird Jim.

We jumped back into bed on the overturned mattress and curled up with the top mat on us and eventually fell asleep again. We were both starkers as we had to take off the wet shirts. I hung the wet sheet on the door to try and dry it before they got up. Something I do to this day. Not peeing the bed. I mean to dry sheets after washing them.

Later, we awoke. I could hear noises downstairs and I was thinking about how I was going to cover up for the wet sheets.

If you remember the movie *Trainspotting* where Spud has heavily shit himself in the bed of a girl he stayed the night with and goes down to see her parents at breakfast and the mum wants to put the sheets in the washer as he told her he peed them... Well, that's what I was like. But no shit, just pee.

While I was thinking, me and wee bro were looking out the bedroom window at the field below. It was new to us seeing all that greenery. The window opened full out so we had a good view. All of a sudden, two boys appeared as it was a lane for a shortcut to the main road. They were in my class at St Mungo's.

"What you doing up there?" they shouted, laughing, "You're dogging school (playing truant)."

At this point, I didn't give a damn about school. I was gonny leave it anyway, but I had more things on my mind at that point...

Next thing, Georgie appeared in the room. She smelt the urine and saw the sheet on the door. She knew at

51

this point what had happened. My brother was crying again.

"I peed the bed," I said, "I'm sorry. I didn't feel myself doing it."

She looked angry but didn't say much, just took everything away and told us to get a bath again. She ran a bath. It was warmer than the night before and she put Dettol in it. We took the damp shirts off and jumped into the bath, which I remember was a warm comfort. She brought us up dry clothes like T-shirts and trousers from our bag we brought with us that Weird Da Jim must have sorted before we came. My bro never asked me at the time why I took the blame. I suppose he was too young. It wasn't important anyway. We didn't get belted for it.

Downstairs, Herman Munster made us toast and tea. They had a butter dish. I had never seen one before. It was glass with a lid on it and had orange jam in another dish, which I didn't like but I got stuck into it anyway. Wee bro didn't eat and had milk. I knew he didn't like milk, which I knew from experience of which I'll bring in later. I made him eat toast and asked them about school and was told there would be no school for now. *Good*, I thought.

All went okay that day considering. Me and wee bro stuck close. I was wondering where my ma was, why we were here and, more important, how long was our stay going to be. I asked, but nobody would say...

Herman Munster was pretty okay. Like he felt sorry for us.

I wanted home. We had nothing to boast about, but it was our home.

That day, Georgie went out. I was aware Herman was in the house with us, but he made us soup. I'll always remember it smelt great. It was homemade.

My brother didn't eat soup. All he ate was beans and they had to be watered down. I told Herman he liked watery beans and he made them as he liked them. He was a decent big guy.

That night, it was back to the bath at 8 p.m., then bed. The night before was now at the back of my mind. It was lights out and we both fell asleep with a full stomach, which was very rare for us.

Later, I woke up. It was dark and I was frozen and bloody wet. Yes, he had peed the bed again. It was like a water slide, but it weren't no amusement park. My brother was crying. He wanted his ma and da.

What do I do now? So, I said, "Right, we stay as we are till it's lighter outside and we fuck off out of here and I'll find our way home."

I never slept but he did. I was planning our escape. Soon as it was light enough, as I was very afraid of the dark, I got him up, dried us both with whatever I could find and got us ready. I grabbed our wee bag of rags and headed downstairs, tiptoeing so as not to be heard.

We got out the door. It was 5:50 a.m. on the kitchen clock. I had an idea how to get home but wasn't a hundred percent sure. Off we ran, down a big hill to the main road. It was very quiet. Once I got to the main road, I was sure I'd get our way.

We walked for ages. Surprised nobody stopped us. I gripped his hand so tight. We were frozen and a bit scared. I wasn't used to seeing the East End at this time in the morning being so young.

54

We walked for what seemed like hours. We were getting weak. Wee bro was sore as his legs were nipping due to him having his own running water tap inside his wee trousers. I eventually recognised where we were: Shettleston. I knew this because I'd been to the old swimming there, even though I'd got there by bus. So, we had about a thirty-minute walk ahead.

I remember being very, very tired and hungry. As we approached Green's Bakers in Westmuir Street, I could smell the newly baked rolls from their ovens. The smell was amazing. Back then, Green's opened at 9 at night. People would queue up and get the fresh hot rolls then jump next door to the chip shop for a large bag of chips. A family of six would go to bed on a full stomach for about five shillings (25p).

I experienced this one cold Sunday night. I was kicking about with a guy called Geordie. He wasn't a regular pal, but it was pissing down and he brought me up to his house at the lower end of my street. His wee ma gave him money to run up to the chip shop. We got the big bag of chips and ran back home. After nicking a few, we tried to get the wrapping newspaper back to the original way.

When we got into his house, his da had buttered bread on plates in front of the big coal fire. He had a couple of kids under him and we all got a warm piece and chips each with brown sauce and a cup of tea. Heaven. I'll never forget that experience.

As a poor family, we never had that experience. We either had the chips and no bread, or the bread and no chips. Never had butter, always had shitty Echo margarine, which was trumped up lard. And never had brown sauce.

All me and wee bro could do was take in the smell to try and fill us up as we hurried on our way. The streets were busy by now as Parkhead had all sorts of steelworks and factories, so men were on their way to work, except Weird Da Jim.

We had all big factories around us. McKellar Watt's, MacFarlane Lang's, Calder Millerfield's, Barr's… all making different types of food or drink. It was murder when you had no money and were hungry. All the aromas around us…

It was like when you'd got a shilling to go to the Granada picture house on a Saturday afternoon matinee. We kept the money we got from bottles on a Friday night. You got two movies. The shit one was always first. You maybe had a few pennies for a sweetie or a penny ice lolly, which was shite, but it kept you cool. Then by the time you were in there, two hours later, you were skint and gagging for a juice. Then the ice cream woman would come around with her tray. It was murder watching all the show-offs getting ice cream or an ice lolly and you were skint. Like best pal Ronnie who always had money, but wouldn't let you lick the ice lolly wrapper. Shithead.

We had our street in our sights now and I was shitting myself. Reality was hitting me hard, and I knew I was in for a good doing (beat up) from Weird Da Jim. How right I was.

The damp was setting in on our clothes, and we must have stunk of urine. I was hoping I never met any pals, or the dafties from Parkhead who used to love beating us up when they caught us. It was like living on a national park full of bampot humans eating each other... like Easterhouse.

The only reason Frankie Vaughan did good for the people of Easterhouse was they told him they would kidnap him and eat him starting with his legs. He later made the song, "There Must Be a Way".

We were now in our close and I hadn't got an excuse as to why we were there. I rattled the loose letterbox. I didn't know what time it was but it was still early. I heard a noise and Weird Da Jim opened the door. He was standing there looking at us, trying to comprehend who we were and what we were doing at the door. He had just been woke up by us. He had a T-shirt on, big baggy underpants and his smelly socks. His eyes where slant due to the shock.

"What the fuck are you doing here? Where's Auntie Georgie? Get in here."

I tried to tell him what happened. Next thing, bang. I had felt this experience all too often. I got punched on the head. He always hit me on the head. I think he hated me actually and wanted to kill me. He was very strong. I was very weak. Great for him, not for me.

I got slapped and punched all over the place, but I would never cry for him. He always held me in a grip on the back of my neck with one hand and knocked the absolute shit out of me with the other hand. Then I'd get thrown into our shit cold bedroom, then I cried, where he couldn't see or hear me, in the shed with the bed.

I just wanted my ma in the house. At least she spoke to me, usually, "Jim, go get me Askit Powders." She was addicted to them I later found out.

Weird Da Jim had a job then and was pissed off because we had turned up. But he was most likely happy now he had an excuse not to go to work.

Couple of days later, my ma appeared. I knew she wasn't well because I used to listen at the bedroom door. She was always in bed. She was in a room with wee Auntie Beattie (aka Toupence). I later found out she was away because she had a miscarriage due to all the Askit Powders she was taking.

Wee Toupence got the aka because she was always running errands for everyone, and always nicked two pennies from their change. Hence, Toupence. Hilarious.

I went back to school and set about getting out of it. I told my ma I kept getting sick and had to come off the bus. By this time, I was dogging it (playing truant) and didn't give a shit. Hanging around Woolworths in town or some days I'd go to Westhorn Park in London Road next to the Celtic club and training ground. No luxuries back then. I'd break into the wee greenhouses in the plots and take whatever I could. One day, I was watching for the park guys going out to commence cutting the grass. I nipped into their office and they had a bowl with blue and white rings. I looked at it and it was full of change. I bagged the money, stole their sandwiches on the table and headed into town. Happy day that day…

I got sent to the doctor and faked everything I could. His diagnosis was I had a liver complaint. *I'll take that, thanks,* I thought, and never went back to the dark ages of St Mungo's and the sadistic men in black cloaks.

I was now getting enrolled into the school for dummies in the East End. I was too good for it, but my pals were there and I was happier. No uniform required.

CHAPTER SEVEN

Weird Da Jim got himself a nightshift job in the McKellar Watt factory in Shettleston. He started at 9 p.m. My ma was working in the pubs and she finished at 10 p.m., so it was arranged I would keep an eye on my brother aged five and my sister aged eighteen months until Ma got home about 10:30. Or so he thought.

By now, she had resigned from the day job at the oatcake factory. He said it was too much for her and now he had the nightshift, there was no need for her to work long hours. She got the choice: give up the day job or give up the pub job. I was to learn very quick as to why she chose to give up the day job.

It was coming up for Christmas. I was eleven and a half. I was thinking Christmas would be good as both parents were working… Not.

I remember Weird Da Jim looking at a toy catalogue and telling me to pick something. I picked a set of two

61

cowboy guns in their holsters and a toy car. My brother picked whatever he picked. All excited, I was thinking, *This is going to be a good Christmas!* I overlooked the fact Weird Da Jim had a major gambling habit on the horses. I was soon to learn the lesson of never assuming...

We had a family upstairs from us who were as poor as us. The dad was grossly overweight. His name, or nickname, was "Beef"... for obvious reasons. They, like us, had nothing. Ma, da and five kids. And a skinny dog.

When I was out playing with my pals, I had to be in for 8 p.m. to let Weird Da Jim get to work. I didn't mind too much as Ma would be in by 10:30ish and would bring in a bag of chips. On a Friday night, she would bring in a jar of Gold Star mixed pickles because she got paid. So, I always made sure the two siblings were asleep before she got in. It was real good for me and my ma to have some precious time together as we always had a good gab. I was so happy then as I was at my new school for morons by this time too and it was only a fifteen-minute walk away. Ma would bring in the chips and I would have the tea ready and the bread buttered. Well, it wasn't butter. It was some shite called Echo margarine. Looked and tasted like cheap lard, but with hot chips on a plain piece of bread, who cared.

Life was going okay, then suddenly Ma wasn't coming home at her usual time. It was midnight. I was always worried. Remember, no phones back then. She would always make an excuse and say, "Don't say to yer da," which I never did. We hardly spoke anyway.

Then it became 1 a.m., then 2 a.m. Remember, we lived in a bottom flat and it was very dark outside. Street lighting was still lit by gas around the East End and was very faint. We used to sit in the living room, which was at the back. We had a coal fire, but coal was scarce, My wee brother was very scared. My sister cried a lot due to being hungry or having a wet nappy. And me? Well, I was terrified that my ma wouldn't come home at all. Weekends were the worst. A lot of drunks would be about.

I remember one night it was about midnight and the electricity went out due to no money in the meter. It took a shilling (5p). I knew we had candles in a cupboard, so I lit a couple. One of them got toppled over and landed on the old couch, which had this kind of cover on it, and caught fire. I ran to the kitchen and got water to put it out.

63

The living room was stinking of the smell, so I opened the window.

About fifteen minutes later, an old guy appeared at the window shouting, "Give me money!"

I screamed and ran upstairs to Big Beef and banged on their door. He sent his wife and daughter down. His daughter was a year older than me. The guy was gone, my brother was crying on the chair and my sister was crying on a makeshift bed I made her on the floor.

Jeanie, the wife, was appalled at what she saw. By now, I was shaking and crying and she sat with us till my ma came home, drunk as usual. Jeanie gave her shit, but back then a lot of neighbours were very loyal to each other. She was one of them, so Weird Da Jim never found out.

Next night, I was out playing and was trying to think of some way to sort this. I was terrified of the next night coming, so I stupidly decided if I wasn't home then Weird Da Jim couldn't go to work and me and my siblings would be safe. So, knowing he was expecting me home at 8 p.m., I decided to just go walking for a long time, then by the time I walked back, it would be too late for him to go to work.

I walked from Parkhead along London Road passed Auchenshuggle towards Mount Vernon. I never knew these places, but as long as I stayed on the main road, I could find my way back. It was very dark and cold, but I was determined to do this. My fear of being in the house again that night was greater than the cold dark road I was on. I walked for what I guessed was a couple of hours then I went home. Bad mistake.

I got dragged in, beaten to a pulp, then he went to work, leaving me battered and crying and now afraid of the hours ahead of me. My brother and sister were crying too. I moved us all into the front room, which had an electric fire. I found milk to heat up for my sister, and bread and sugar for my brother. I was hoping the electric would last and I didn't light candles again. I remember my ear being very sore and I kept hearing a noise in it. I'd had a perforated ear drum from birth and when Weird Da Jim whacked me on the side of the head, it opened it up and made it worse. I was in agony.

I managed to change my sister's nappy and she was able to fall asleep. My brother fell asleep and I was sitting alone, listening for noises, as you do. Because we were now in the front room, I could hear everything outside. Stray dogs and cats were always about and rats were in big supply. I heard this noise coming from the living room and my heart was pumping like mad.

I went out to the hall and shouted, "Who's there? I have a metal bar."

No noise was heard. I opened the door and looked into the dark living room. It was all quiet, so I went back into the front room. I was shaking with fear.

Ten minutes or so later, I heard a bang at the window. I panicked and ran upstairs to Jeanie, again banging on her door crying. She came down and nobody was around. She told her daughter to sit with us, but she was scared too.

Later that day, Jeanie had been down at our house. She must have warned my ma about what was going on, and Ma stopped working from that day. It worked out she was having a fling with her boss and was away with him in his car after work till all hours.

I resented her for the rest of her life for putting me through that fear. I ended up having to see a counsellor when I was forty years old for that and the beatings I took. None of which I deserved. But that spell of fear was haunting me to the point I was drinking too much at the time. I could not come to terms with why I hated my mother so much, yet my two brothers and two sisters all loved her, and they turned against me for this. They never knew what I went through and when I tried to tell them, they said I was imagining it, but also, I wasn't their real brother either. So, a gap was there too.

I tried to talk to a counsellor, but it was very upsetting and I would bawl my eyes out and feel so guilty. I never went back and just dealt with it as best I could. I thought I was going mad at a point and started being a really angry drunk. Shame, because I am a real nice guy, like I was when I was a kid.

CHAPTER EIGHT

Two weeks till Christmas and my ma had no job. The bold boy had been in a fight at work and lost his job. Now we were back in the shit we crawled out of. But, on the bright side, Christmas was coming and I had my guns to get and my car. And also, I had got a wee crap cassette thing that only played one song called, "Oh, Suzanna, why don't you cry for me…"

Two days before Christmas, I came into the house and it was all dark.

"What's wrong?" I asked.

Ma was crying. "Lecky has been cut aff, son."

"What do you mean?"

"Nae money for meter and I owe them money."

Now, back then, they were ruthless. No matter who was young or infirm, if you didn't pay, it was cut off. So, there we were: no money, no lecky, no coal for the fire, no money coming in and Christmas only a fucking day away. My pals were asking what I was getting…

Christmas Day arrived. I was up like a lark, all excited, frozen also, but excited. Weird Da Jim gave me a holster with one gun and no car. My bro had one gun and a car. After disputing this, I was told that due to no money, instead of me getting my two guns in a holster, I got one and my brother got the other.

"No chance," I shouted.

I grabbed his gun and left him with the car, crying. I ran out to meet my pals with my two guns in the proper holsters. Who did I meet first, but greedy best pal Ronnie and a couple of others.

"Look," I shouted, holding my two cowboy guns in the air, all excited.

Ronnie asked, "What you doing getting toys? We all got clothes for Christmas this year. You're too old now for toys."

My head fell as fast as my heart, and they were all laughing at me. Bastards. I'll never forget that miserable day. Then, of course, to make it more exciting, we had bananas for Christmas dinner that day, as I explained earlier…

I never went out to play for a couple of days. I went to visit my uncle James and my aunt Beattie, aka Toupence. Uncle James was my godfather. He was very good to me. Always called me "kid". I wished so much he was my dad. Turned out, him and my ma were inseparable when they were kids. They were half brother and sister, then Uncle James got sent to Borstal, then into the RAF. He never liked my real da, Pat, or Weird Da Jim. To be honest, I think he loved my ma.

Him and Toupence always had a wee gift for me, for me only, but they had three kids and I didn't like to get between them all at Christmas, but I just loved Uncle James. I miss him to this day, and if there is an afterlife, I want to meet Uncle James. Died aged fifty-two. My ma died aged eighty. My brother died aged nine months. My real da, Pat, died aged sixty-five, and my son Paul passed away at birth on 17th January 1975 and we can all have a laugh and be happy and let the living all get on with it. Wee Toupence is still living. She married a wee guy called Bob. Now "bob" is the short name for a shilling, so I used to call them One- and Toupence, which was the old name for one shilling and two pennies…

CHAPTER NINE

Hogmanay arrived and it had been snowing. Back then, it always snowed at Christmas and New Year. We still had no electricity and by now getting used to the cosiness of the candles and the bit of heat they gave off. The couch still bore the scars of the previous episode, but my ma had covered them with a sheet. We had nothing. Skint, hungry and sad.

Anyone who mentions the "good old days" makes me cringe. People will say, "Well, it never done us any harm." It didn't? Well, where the hell were you brought up because it's harmed me for life. Idiots.

At the bells, midnight, the door went. It was Big Beef, Jeanie and the kids. He had some whisky and two bottles of beer and shortbread. Now, here's what puzzled me. Rewind back to Christmas Day.

I came home totally pissed off with best pal spoilt Ronnie, and the mob of his followers, about my guns. I was sitting on the stairs just plain fed up of being let down and embarrassed and Jeanie's oldest daughter Margaret came down and sat beside me. Remember, it was her who got sent to sit with me in the house of terror when my ma was neck stretching a guy's chicken (work that one out) in his car at 2 in the morning.

"How's things?" she asked.

I sat and told her my story of the day.

She said, "Don't feel so bad, at least you got something."

I looked at her and asked, "What do you mean? We got nothing at all."

She said, "My da said Santa was only giving to the poor in Africa this year."

Jesus Christ, she floored me. Now, she was twelve, but her siblings were all Santa believers and she started crying. It didn't make me feel better. I got angrier, realising this poor family were worse than us. How could this be? I thought we were the poorest in the street. Then, of course, there was my pal Ikey. He got nothing too, but that was normal for him. He just accepted the fact and never showed any feelings on it.

So, getting back to the Hogmanay scenario. I was thinking, *Where did he get the money for this when his kids had no toys?* I never got the answer to that. Poor kids. I sat in disgust that night, in the flicking ambience of four cheap candles and a half-lit smelly smoky coal fire…

Couple of days later, I was still staying in due to being embarrassed about my shit guns. Pals all got new clothes for Christmas. I got two… sorry, one gun for mine. If it had been a real one, I would have shot them all and stole their new clothes.

I heard a loud scream in the entry to our houses. I ran out and saw Jeanie's second youngest daughter, who was about seven years old, crying.

I asked, "What's up?"

She said, "That man touched me."

I looked out and saw this wee kinda bald guy running away. He was overweight and wearing an overcoat.

I said, "Run up and get your ma and da and tell them."

75

I bolted out after him and down the street. I saw an empty bottle lying en route, so I picked it up and continued after him.

At the bottom of the street, he had to stop. He was panting and sweating. I stopped, looked him in the eye and smashed the bottle over his head. All the anger I had in me came out. He went down a bit, grabbing hold of the fence behind him, but looked and saw a few people running down towards us. He bolted as fast as I've ever seen anyone running, head bleeding. He knew they would have beat the shit out of him. Nobody called the cops then. They dealt with it accordingly.

The neighbours were all asking me what happened. I looked up the street and saw the overweight figure of Beef trying to make it towards us. His big massive tent sized shirt was all hanging out. He was sweating.

I felt a euphoria. At last, I was everyone's hero.

Big Beef put his massive arms around me. I'll never forget the smell of his hairy pits on my face. My ma appeared and gave me trouble after hearing what I done to the guy, but Beef and Jeanie cut her off saying I saved their daughter from a pervert. Back then, word got about very fast. Well, we never had Freeview and Sky TV to occupy our boring lives…

I couldn't wait to go back out to meet my so-called pals. Now they were all asking what happened and how mad (East End for "brave") I was. Greedy Ronnie was so jealous. I loved it. In fact, his wee da gave me two shillings the next day and said, "Well done, son, you should have killed the bastard."

I was a hero and I loved it. The shit Christmas and New Year were well out of my mind by now.

CHAPTER TEN

I carried on business as usual after that: running errands and trying to make money. Summer had come and I was twelve and gaining attitude.

My ma had popped another child: a boy. He was always crying. He had a skin problem, always itchy with sores weeping. Poor kid. I used to help Ma to get his nappy off and his wee vest. He would be screaming in agony as the sores would come away with his clothes. He was in and out of hospital. It took me back to my wee brother who died, but this went on for a couple of years.

Eventually, they found a cream, named Quinoderm, and it helped him a lot. He's fifty now and has the most perfect skin on any man. Goes as brown as chocolate in the sun. I'm glad for him. Only thing is, he has a wandering eye, or lazy eye as they call it. It's all over the fucking place. When he cries, the tears run down his back at times. More about him later...

I was doing okay at my school for morons. As I approached thirteen, they noticed I had a brain, so they split the classes of this age into two. You got assessed by the teachers and the decent ones got put into engineering, and the dafties (morons) got put into building. I was in engineering. It was good. We did metalwork and made metal things of no use to man nor beast. When you made something and showed it to people, the same question was asked: "What the fuck is that?"

It gave me an insight into engineering, but I secretly wished I was with the dafties making things in woodwork and the like. If they made a stool, which was popular back then, everyone knew it was a stool... even though it sat slant.

They also got wallpapering and painting, which I fancied as I always watched my ma do all this in the house, when she could afford it, to cover all the drawings I used to put on the living room walls. She would wait till we were all in bed and set about the place and have it all done before we got up. She was very smart. I took a lot of my skills and abilities from her that got me through life. Weird Da Jim was heart lazy and did nothing in the house. Well, he made a few dents on the walls with my head... or with his fist when I ducked to miss one.

At thirteen, I started to look for better ways to make money. No more running errands for neighbours. I got a part-time job in a fruit and veg shop for a guy and his sister, John and Nan. I loved it. It was a busy shop at weekends, so I learnt the ways very quick and I started to do the counter facing customers. I found I had good manners and, more importantly, good patter. Customers loved me, plus I would throw in the odd bit extra for the poorer people I knew. Again, a trait I took from my ma who, remember, worked in the pubs where you needed to be sharp tongued...

Not long after we were back in the shit as a family, Weird Da Jim wasn't working again. Ma was pregnant again and lying in bed all day with wee Toupence in the house every day looking after her and going for her Askit Powders, which she was back on. Plus, nicking the odd pennies, I guess.

Now the pressure was on me again. I was giving my ma all the bits of money I was earning, then I started nicking fruit and veg for the family. We were starving and had nothing. Very soon, I got caught and booted up the arse and tossed out the shop. Now what did I do?

I started hanging out with older boys as well as a few I knew from school. A few girls started tagging along too. Most of them had an eye for greedy best pal Ronnie. It didn't bother me that much. He was almost a year older than me, and because everyone knew his brother had the boys' gate open for anyone to enter, he was terrified he would get the same reputation.

I had lacked confidence due to not having any money or the nice clothes they all were starting to wear, so to get attention I started to be the idiot to gain street credit. If there was a way to steal, I'd be first in. If we were gonny do a shop, I was first to boot the doors in… at least try. The adrenaline rush was great and I got noticed. But I still took shit because of my status in life, i.e. shit clothes and plastic shoes with holes in them. God only knows how I stood up to this.

My ma got me these trousers. I was coming on thirteen. I put them on and thought they would cover the burst shoes I was wearing. That night, some smart arse noticed they were girls' trousers, and also the torn shoes. Well, I got it from every direction that summer's night. Greedy Ronnie (best pal) got in on it too. I decided that night he was no longer my best pal, but I had an ace up my sleeve…

I knew a big guy from kicking about the East End streets named Martin. Older than me by a year. He was a quiet guy and seemed okay. His older brother Danny was weird. Used to cause a rumpus, fight with neighbours, then disappear for months. Then he'd come back and do the same again. Thing was, he never went anywhere, just stayed in the house. He had a younger brother, Shugie. He was strange too. Nobody ever knew much about Shugie until he met a strange girl, and by seventeen had two kids. Not that strange, eh!

His mum and dad were quiet living people. In fact, they all were. So, Martin and me started being pals. He was a good guy, introduced me to music of many types. The Beach Boys were his favourite. I got to know his parents pretty good. They liked me and Martin never judged me on my clothes or status. He knew of me, I later learnt. We became really good pals. I was thirteen, he was fourteen. Both Taureans. He was May 3rd, I was May 7th.

Martin was a big solid-built guy. A big gentle giant. One night, we were out hanging with some girls. It was a summer night, school holidays.

At 8 p.m., my wee brother found me and said, "Da wants you home."

I said, "Bugger off. Say you couldn't find me."

But earlier I said they were not my real brothers and sisters. Well, it showed big time as he told Weird Da Jim what I said.

One of the girls said, "Hey, Jimmy, yer old man is coming."

Big Martin knew of him through stories I'd told him.

Martin said, "Fuck off, Jim. He will calm down later."

I stood my ground. Remember, I said I had an ace up my sleeve regarding ex-best pal Ronnie? Well, he was ugly in looks and I was becoming a really good-looking young kid. In summer, I tanned so dark so fast, so I got major attention from the girls. Older ones too. He hated this. He was so, so jealous...

Due to the girls being present, I wasn't running. Weird Da Jim came to me. It was at the old tenements in Dechmont Street and Springfield Road in Parkhead. He grabbed me by the usual part of my body, my neck, dragged me into a close and beat the shit out of me. I got kicked, punched and tossed against the wall. Punch after punch came onto me.

My pals shouted, "Leave him, you bastard."

Big Martin jumped on him with a girl called Jean, but he spun them off. A man and woman got involved of who I never knew.

They said, "You're a bully hitting that boy."

I was still a skinny wee guy.

It was all because he wanted me to go for his sweets. He would never go to the shops for anything. Only the betting shop to bet on the horses.

He let me go. I was throbbing, but again I would not cry for him. My nose was bleeding quite bad, I had a bruised eye and again my ear was sore. My shoulder felt as if it was broken. All the shit and beatings I took was because I wasn't his son…

Now at this stage in my life, I had a paper run delivering around the locals and making a few bob. I saved enough to buy a cheaper version of an Arthur Black shirt. Arthur Blacks were very expensive. You designed your own shirt, but I was very proud of the cheaper one I saved up to buy. It was lime green with black stitching, and with my tan and being slim (skinny, underfed), I looked the part. I only put it on that day and the girls loved it. I was all proud… Well, the bully bastard ripped the collar right off it by pulling me about.

When he stopped hitting me, he said, "Get home. You're not getting back out."

But I seen the look he gave me. He got a fright when he saw what he had done. So, him and me walked the ten-minute walk back home. Big Martin and the others were shouting abuse to him while keeping their distance from him. I walked slow as my lower back was sore. I didn't know if he kneed me, kicked me or punched me in that area.

On the way, he said, "Why didn't you come when I sent your brother for you?"

I never answered him. I knew if I spoke, I would break down. I never answered him…

Back in the house, he went to his chair. He had sent my brother for his sweets and he started munching on them. I went into my ma's room and got the sewing box and found a needle and thread. I went back into the living room and sat on the filthy sofa we had and started trying to sew my collar on. A trait from my school days with the gym uniform I tried to sew. I never spoke a word to him.

Eventually, he said sorry.

I kept my mind on the sewing.

He said, "You made me angry."

I looked at him and said, "Fuck you. Wait till I tell Auntie Jean. You can try and beat her up."

Now his expression changed. He knew what she was like (remember old Granda's funeral and Mary the Tinker earlier?) and he also knew what she was like with me. I was her favourite. She gave me more attention than she did with her own son.

87

Now, Weird Da Jim could handle himself. He feared no man, but Auntie Jean was different. First, she was a woman. Back then, if you hit a woman, you had to move out of the area. Fast. Secondly, she fought like an animal, and if you put her down, she kept coming back and back and back, until she tore your eyes out. I've seen her take on a man and beat him. She beat up Mary the Tinker, and that was big news. Everyone feared Auntie Jean. With the booze in her, even the cops feared her and came in numbers to deal with her. She had black eyes and pale skin and, in a temper, she was like a lion with a thorn in its side.

I got up and went into the bedroom. Now I was feeling the pains and the embarrassment of getting beat up in front of everyone. I cried myself to sleep that night.

My ma was working the pubs again by this time as he was in his lazy mode. He must have told her when she got in that night. She came in and woke me up. I had a black eye, dried blood on my face and I ached all over. She went away and I heard a bawling argument and doors banging. I assumed that both of them knew what was coming. I just lay there in the dark, wishing for the day I could leave school, get my own clothes and fuck the lot of them. My new shirt was also ruined, which pissed me right off. If my shirt was okay, maybe I would not have said anything to Auntie Jean, just to save my wee ma a lot of grief, but this needed to be made public. A storm was coming…

CHAPTER ELEVEN

I lost my paper run due to a local bully who was notorious in the area. He wanted my paper run and I wasn't arguing with him. Big Martin helped an uncle out who had a business, so he always had a few bob. He was good with me and bought me the odd bag of chips and Irn-Bru or sweets.

I started just sitting in his room with him at night if it was raining, listening to music and looking at LPs and stuff. He had a big black tom cat. You could smell it in the house. I didn't have much time for greedy Ronnie or his new cronies. Me and Big Martin got on great. Really good pals. I stayed out of trouble too...

It was Friday. I was home from school and looking forward to the weekend. The door banged and it was

Auntie Jean. She was in good spirits and gave me a big hug and a chocolate bar, and sweets for the siblings. I noticed she had gin in her bag also. *Trouble ahead*, I thought.

"Right, Maggie. Let's go tae the pub."

Ma said, "No, Jean, I can't. I have to work tonight."

She knew later that night Auntie Jean would turn up at the pub. It was a tough pub in the Calton area. At weekends, Auntie Jean would be there to watch my ma's back and tackle any drunks who got mouthy with her. My ma was the youngest of seven sisters.

The gin came out and the party began. We ate our sweets and listened to Auntie Jean's stories, and she had many. I went out later, about 6.

I came in and Auntie Jean was pished. Ma was away to work. Weird Da Jim was in alone with her. I walked into the living room.

Jean shouted, "Come here, you. I want to speak to you."

I was shitting myself, but I didn't know why. Yet…

"Let me look at you," she shouted, grabbing me very rough.

Now, I saw her fight, saw her drunk, but never heard her swearing. She was holding me by the collar and swung me round towards Weird Da Jim.

"Look, you basket (her term for bastard). You gave this boy a beating, did you? He's my boy. Nobody hits him and gets away with it."

She threw me on the couch and pulled up her skirt in an instant. I thought, *That's weird.* She jumped on him on his chair. It was so fast. She was screaming like a monster, scratching and biting and punching him while pulling his hair. He never expected it so fast. He had to act or she would have killed him.

He got up, but she was clinging to him, biting him. I saw blood. He was dragging her off of him, but she wouldn't let go, still punching him and scratching him. I was screaming at her to let go. The kids were all crying with fear. Furniture was broken and the old TV was smashed.

The next-door neighbour's son came in with a big guy and tried to separate them. Auntie Jean was exhausted, but still trying to fight. Her eyes were crazy-looking, but she was losing strength.

93

They finally got her down. He was badly cut all over and white with anger.

She got up, grabbed her coat and bag, looked at me in the eye with her black eyes and said, "That basket will never touch you again, son."

And you know what? That was the last time he ever put a finger on me. Turned out, my ma told her what happened. I'm glad she did. She later headed to the pub my ma worked at to tell her what happened. She ended up beating up a woman and a guy that night who argued with my ma about wrong change she had given. A good Friday for Auntie Jean. Three people's blood on her hands in one day.

She was about five feet two inches and weighed, I think, approximately seven stone, (a hundred pounds). A fearless animal with the heart of a lion and the most loving generous person you could meet. If she liked you. God bless her. RIP.

CHAPTER TWELVE

I was kind of enjoying the school for morons. The teachers were as whacky as some of the pupils, but more relaxed.

There's something about Catholic priests, nuns, brothers of the so-called faith being teachers. Personally, I think they brainwash more than teach. There is no halfway line, no debate. It's their way or the highway, or a good beating. Or worse, as it was back then. They all assumed wrongly (as we now know) that they were protected by the stinking sweaty cloth they wore and protected by God. Bullshit! I was just glad to be rid of those sadists, and I vowed to myself on that day I left that crap school for the intelligent and the privileged, if I had kids, they would never be taught by any of their types.

I'd started hanging out with some of the East End kids I knew, and some I didn't know, like Goggie McGunn, big Eddie Little, wee Barra Terry Wilson of whom I worked with later in life. A whole bunch of characters. Ex-best pal jealous Ronnie was now out of the frame. He had moved up in the world. Or so he thought. Remember he was one year older.

I was enjoying the crack with the guys and the teachers, although we had one of the brother's teaching, McCormack. He had a booze problem. And the head was an old fucker brother also, called Brother John. He hated everything and everyone, so he was too pre-occupied to bother me.

I got into tech class, bit of woodwork and metalwork, more hands on. Also, we got chemistry. I again got put into a higher class of morons. A class of high hopes and low results. I kind of stood out a bit, made a reputation and I got put into a higher class again. So, now I was with guys a bit older again. Ex-pal Ronnie was in the same year and didn't appreciate me moving up as he wasn't very bright at all. I later found out he got the second lowest mark in his class. He hated me knowing this.

We had an old chemistry teacher they called old Happie, aka Mr Hapworth. Deaf as a post and a hot temper. I had no interest in chemistry. In fact, the previous school knocked the shit out of me in regards to learning.

I had no interest in anything I didn't enjoy doing, but excelled in the things I liked. Like playing truant, amongst others.

One day, we were in class waiting on old Happie coming in. I got hold of a couple of smoke bombs the previous day from a guy. I stuck them in the cupboard under the test bench and lit them just before Happie came in. Smoke was billowing out when he walked in. We were all laughing our heads off. He was going mad and shouting. He never found out who did it. Thank God.

We also had a history teacher called Benny the Bum Feeler. Obese guy with glasses on. Now, I had no interest at all in history, but I kept my eyes firmly on him. I never witnessed this personally, but he was known to drop things and order you to pick them up saying he couldn't bend down. But, if you bent down, he would touch you on the arse. Well, he wasn't touching my arse. Never. I did see him take a blonde guy called Alec, who was quiet and got bullied a bit, away into a room for some "instruction", but who knows what happened...

I know for sure in the late sixties, when I was at school, all sorts were happening with dodgy teachers. I made sure nothing ever happened to me in that sense. I had experienced enough fear in my young life without any of that shit happening to me. Violence was bad enough without having the fear of old Benny using your rear end as a finger dip.

Any teacher who came near me sexually, I would have stabbed them without thinking of it. Fear makes you take desperate measures. You don't plan or think, you strike in panic. It's you or them. I can understand why nowadays a lot of kids who have been in homing centres and the like are unruly and violent. It's the fear they experience in their miserable young lives. It's a shame. Some learn the lesson when it's too late, when they have been sentenced to life for murder or similar. I'm sure they lie in their cell the first night of their sentence and cry their eyes out thinking it's not their fault they have ended up there. Yes, they committed the crime, but who caused the damage in their thinking process when they were young to drive them to do this? But also, some of them are just fucking bonkers and deserve to be where they are…

I started hanging with the wrong ones at school, trying to be as cocky as the older ones and sometimes thrown in the loop of destruction. I found myself hanging out with a gang of bullies at school until one day I saw them giving the quiet blonde boy Alec a hiding for nothing. Poor guy just got up, dusted himself down and walked on, just like I did when I got the hiding from you know who in front of my pals.

At that point, I disconnected from them. I was sick of what they did to this quiet troubled boy. Next day, I apologised to him for being with them, even though I did not take part in the exercise. He just looked at me and walked away.

I later found out he had a very poor upbringing with his grandparents and an older brother who was as quiet as he was. Very sad. I've never forgotten that guy. He still lives in the East End as a loner and I believe he's never held a job. Maybe to do with the bullying, and I was a part of that. I'm ashamed of myself. Thing is, he was blonde and a good-looking kid. If some confidence was instilled in him, he would have been up there with the girls.

That was when I started dogging school (playing truant). I'd just lost interest. St Mungo's for the well-off scarred me. I became a moron. My intelligence put away for another day. I went into self-destruct mode. Getting up to no good, breaking into shops and the odd house, hanging out in odd houses playing cards with older guys I didn't know, just bumbling along with whoever was there.

Weird Da Jim was working. I now had three siblings, but paid no interest in any of them. My ma was working the pubs, coming in late now and then, but I didn't give a shit by then as I knew I wasn't going to school the next day. My focus was getting money to survive the day. I didn't think any further.

Summer holidays were spent stealing and fighting in the gang, experimenting with alcohol, just aged thirteen. I also had a paper run with jealous Ronnie again. It was a good run, but needed two of us. Big Martin was there too, trying to keep me on the straight and narrow, but he wasn't there enough to hold me. I was going to record sessions on a Friday or Saturday night, depending who was having one. I was always the youngest there, but often caught the eye of an older girl.

I started hanging out with a guy called Mowser, aka John Taylor. Mowser came from him being as creepy as a cat. He was disturbed mentally. No parents in his life. They could not cope with him, so a wee aunt got lobbed with him. He had some sick ideas in his head.

He asked me to go with him to the old Belvidere Hospital as his da was a patient there. It wasn't far, so I went. It was a summer's day and the patients were out on open balconies.

As we entered the grounds towards the balconies, he said, "There's the old bastard up there."

He waved to him and his da waved back. We climbed up the wall and over the metal railing fence onto the balcony where a few beds were. We went towards his old man draped in hospital issue striped pyjamas. He looked to me as if he was bending over to hug his da, then all of a sudden, he leant towards him and bit him on the face and would not release the gripping bite. His da was screaming and punching at him, then I saw blood.

I shouted, "Mowser, for fuck's sake, the nurses are coming."

He let his bite go, lifted his head and laughed. He looked like a vampire, mouth all blood.

His da was screaming.

We bolted over the wall and ran like shit outta there. Later, I asked him why he did this.

He said, "I never got a kiss from any of my parents, so I've just gave the old fucker a kiss he won't forget all his life. And when I see my ma, I'll do the same to her."

I decided from then I didn't like Mowser.

We were to cross paths a year later when he attacked me in Shettleston with a knife, hitting me several times on the back when I was on the ground. Luckily, it was blunt and didn't do much damage. Well, physically anyway. All because he heard I was talking to a girl he was going about with. A week later, he apologised to me. About three years later, he got stabbed to death in the East End in a pub fight. No great loss in my book. He most certainly would have moved on to do a lot of damage to a lot of people. I just hoped he never got to kiss his mum.

You know that feeling when you've been constipated for two weeks, then all of a sudden, what's in there just releases and disappears down the toilet. Pure relief, you think to yourself. Well, his parents and the wee auntie must have had that experience of relief when Mowser died. Certainly his dad "Tommy Two Face" must have had. That's what his mum should have done to him at birth: doon the pan wi him.

CHAPTER THIRTEEN

Being back on tour with jealous Ronnie doing the paper runs was okay. On a Saturday, we had the football newspapers, The Glasgow Times and The Citizen, which had a colour souvenir special: a full-size colour photo of the star players with each issue. One weekend, it was Celtic at Parkhead. Next week, it was Rangers at Ibrox. It was great fun.

On a Saturday, we would count all our money up in the snooker hall in Parkhead. We did the souvenir specials before the game. We rushed to get The Times' half-time results in the pubs and in the stadiums. Then we'd rush again to get the full-time results edition and go in and out the pubs again. Everyone did the football pools then and were keen to get the results. Back then, there was no crowd control. Everyone packed in. They would then open the gates at half time and let more people in for free. Until the awful Ibrox disaster on 2nd January 1971, Rangers versus Celtic.

People were leaving early to catch a bus or go to the pub or whatever their reason. Celtic were leading 1:0. In the last minutes, Colin Stein scored to equalise and all hell broke loose. Everyone tried to get back up the stairs against all who were leaving and 66 people died, 200-odd injured. Over 80,000 fans crammed in. Rangers were liable and all rules changed due to this for the better.

Back to Saturday night at Alien Snooker Club and we had the money counted. I had money in my pocket and was mixing with the older gang.

At the local off-sales, we would hang around the doorway, waiting for older guys going in for a carry out, and asking them to get us a bottle of wine. I don't mean Tesco's Finest Merlot. No, it was Eldorado or Barchester or Lanliq. All cheap and strong and great to get us all pished. Well, when you're thirteen, the smell walking by a pub would make you drunk. We would all get drunk and party.

I started hanging out in a notorious area called Camlachie at Barrowfield in the East End, where the Forge

Shopping Centre is now, with a gang called the Torch. It was a whole new experience. A new real gang. A few of us ventured there to join: me, jealous Ronnie, Fedaro Farley, wee Jamie White and a couple of others whose names have escaped me. A guy called Rab Weir and his girlfriend Ann were the leaders.

Me and Rab hit it off right away. We got on really well. We were up to all sorts, like street urchins run by Fagan. No school, stealing scrap from the empty tenements, breaking into the old shops along the Gallowgate... We mugged the wee postman a few times and broke into his wee Morris Minor car stealing the parcels. Up in the old tenements, we would go and rip out the block tin from the walls, which carried electric cables, and rip out the lead and copper piping. If football was on at Celtic Park on a Wednesday night and it was dark, we would lie in wait in the dark back courts and catch the mugs who would take the shortcuts to catch a bus and rob them of anything they had. Now I wasn't selling newspapers for money. We were in a gang and we looked after each other. Nobody starved. I loved it...

Rab was a cocky character. He wasn't violent as such. That's why he had Ann as his bird. She was the violent one. But he was so funny a guy.

One day, I got home at the usual time. My ma was in the kitchen and Weird Jimbo was raging mad.

"How was school?" he shouted.

I looked at them both and said, "Aye, it's okay."

"You're a liar," he said and belted me, bang, right across his favourite part, my head. "You've no been at school for five days."

I picked myself up from the floor and gave a silent laugh as I hadn't been at school for six weeks. *I'll take the punch for that*, I thought.

I had to go back to school. The school board issued me with a card that had to be signed every day by a teacher. I was coming on fourteen by this time and I didn't give a shit about anything except my gang.

Anyway, I was back at school and a wee pal of mine called Slippy Eddie told me about some big guy at school who had loads of money every day. Big Tam Willouby. Built like a shithouse but thick as mud. Turned out, I knew him. Not great, but it was a start. He lived near Torchland, but didn't get involved with gangs. Wanted to, but wasn't allowed. Well, that was our start. Me and Slippy made friends with Big Tam. He knew I ran about Camlachie and envied me. Slippy came from Carntyne, the other end of the East End. He was a character like Rab.

Turned out, Big Tam's sister's husband had won the pools. Massive win. Life-changing win. Well, banks then were not like today. Nobody bothered with them, in the East End anyway. We had fuck all to put in them, so why visit them?

So, Tam's sister had given her mum wads of cash, so much she didn't know how much she was giving her. Her mum never had a clue how much she had, so Big Tam was dipping her overflowing purse every morning with handfuls of one pound notes. Me and Slippy became his best pals. I couldn't believe my luck. The positive in this was my school attendance was A1. No way was I missing school for this windfall.

Every day he was on the money, we would go to the shops and Tam would buy everything. On a Friday, it was chip shop day, like the time at St Mungo's with my Friday chip shop experience. It was pie suppers or fish suppers or fritters. Also, we drank the best gingers to wash it all down. Big Tam didn't give a shit. He knew we were using him, but he had two good pals to hang out with.

Eventually, as you do, you want to venture out in the world. We decided to dodge school and head for the city centre. By now, penny arcades with one arm bandits and snooker halls were popping up, so that's where we headed. Also, Woolworths had opened a big sit-in restaurant in Argyle Street.

One day, we were up to get a fish tea. We were sitting at our table and the woman brought the condiments over. The waitresses had uniforms and wee petticoat type aprons, all nice. Our grub came and always my first move was the vinegar. I'm still the same today.

Slippy grabbed the salt dish and we were whacking it all over our meal. Tam grabbed a big jar thing with white stuff in it and a spout with a wee lip on the spout. He poured it all over his fish and chips. Now, before this, we

110

had been in the amusements and lost all our share of the money with only enough to buy our food.

I was looking in shock. Slippy hadn't noticed.

I shouted, "Tam, ya bam, what you doing?"

He looked at me. He had a lazy eye, as well as a lazy body, and said, "What's wrong?" as he slipped a forkful of chips in his mouth.

I said, "You've just poured sugar all over your dinner." I was pissing myself laughing.

Just as he was starting to munch his chips, he realised his error and spat everything all over us and the white linen table cover. He started crying and started wiping the sugar off of his dinner.

Slippy said, "Ah, stop moaning. Just put it all on yer piece and eat it."

Tam couldn't eat it, but Slippy Eddie did. All of it, sugar and all.

We also got thrown out for the mess. Hilarious.

We had to walk home that day. Overspent Tam's money...

CHAPTER FOURTEEN

I was going from bad to worse. I went back to school, but school was not important to me now. In a year, I would be leaving, at fifteen years old, get a job, have money of my own and, most importantly, I'd stop taking orders from Weird Da Jim as to when I came home or going to shops for his sweets. I didn't give a shit. Only my mates in the gang counted and, by now, the girls too…

Rab's girlfriend Ann, as I said before, had a crazy temper. One night when I wasn't there, they were mugging fans from the Wednesday night game. This guy apparently put up resistance and had a fight with Ann. She pulled her weapon of choice on him, a steel comb with a tail, and stuck it into him in a rage. The poor guy lost his life. She went into hiding, but her sister turned her in. She got life and did nine years. She was fifteen. Thank God I wasn't there.

We carried on as usual, as you do. Got pissed at weekends, back dogging school and another sibling had arrived back at the house.

My ma now had a phone. A big mustard thing it was. One morning, it was ringing. It was the school. But by now I was getting smart. I practised writing the teacher's signature on my dogging card and started signing it myself. She was shouting at me that I was to go to the school with her and Weird Da Jim. No chance!

While she was on the phone, I slipped into the toilet, escaped out of the window and offskied back along to Camlachie. It was a frosty morning. I remember I slipped on my arse running away. I got to Rab's house. He had left school by now, but had no interest in finding a job. He was a petty thief, that was his job, and I wanted to be like him.

"Nae problem," he said, "Crash at mine."

Rab had two younger brothers and a sister, so I stayed at his. Slept in the bunk beds: him at one end, me at the other.

Next day, we were up early and out, trying to find a money source. The postman had his car parked on

Gallowgate and he was away up to deliver letters. We scanned his car and there were parcels in it. We bricked the window, grabbed the stuff and bolted. We knew the wee guy. He was old and couldn't run, and he knew what would happen to him if he caused us grief anyway. But running was the buzz and apart from the money, the adrenaline buzz was brilliant.

We sorted our blag; a few items we decided could be pawned. Back then, the pawnshop took anything, so that was what we'd do. But the pawnshop was down in Spur land, extreme enemy territory, so we had to be careful. These guys would chib you, which in Glasgow means attack you with a knife until you're severely injured. It was all about street cred. You carried what they did to you on your body for the rest of your life. Not like a tattoo. I mean, heavy scars. You go anywhere in Glasgow to this day and you will see hundreds, maybe thousands, of guys and girls with big scars, usually on the face where it can't be hidden, called a chib mark. Or some call it a second prize, which meant you lost the fight.

It was decided that I would go in with the stuff. We had been to this pawn before with previous knock-offs.

Rab was barred from it for arguing about a price of something and giving the guy abuse. So, I went in with the few things, one of which was a brolly. Can you imagine doing that now?

I went into the wee cubicle for privacy, mostly in case I was seen by someone I didn't want to see. The young girl came over to me and I handed over the stuff.

"Just give me what it's worth to you," I said.

"What's your name?"

I said, "Ikey Dymock." Remember wee poor Ikey? The girl looked at me. "What's yer address?"

"200 Janefield Street," I said.

"How's my auntie Sally?" she asked.

I was struck dumb.

"Get out, you thieving fuck, don't come back."

I later found out she was a cousin of Ikey's. Turned out, the reason she asked about Auntie Sally was Ikey's old violent da died about a year before this and she was at his funeral. So, we had a bad day that day.

Later that Friday night, we needed to get money. Friday night was party night. We decided to do a shop when they closed and we picked a wee hardware shop on the Gallowgate. We had a fence called Lackie who bought stuff from us, but not brollies. We got in the doorway and kicked in the inner door to the open shop. I can always remember the smell of old wooden counters and shelves and stuff. It was dark.

Rab said, "Go upstairs and find a box to put stuff in."

I scrambled up the wooden stairs in the dark with my heart pounding. I could hear Rab opening drawers looking for cash.

Next thing I heard was, "Who's there?" It was the cops. We were done for.

I noticed a window and opened it. I scrambled down the ledge and off I went.

Back at Camlachie, I was telling a few of the lads. We found out from Rab's wee ma he'd been lifted, arrested, and he was in the nick. Cops had been at his house. What did I do? I got pissed. The guys had a carry out. We always went up the railway arches to drink in case cops got us for underage drinking. I told Rab's wee brother Joe about my plight: Rab in the nick and I'd no bed.

Joe said, "It's okay. Sneak in with me later."

So, we were hanging over the railway arch looking down at the poorly lit streets and a car pulled up. I knew the car. It was a neighbour's. Who was in it? Weird Da Jim and the neighbour, who originally came from Camlachie and knew most of the dafties, but not the younger dafties who I was involved with.

One of the guys lobbed a big stone at the car then we all pissed over the wall on top of it, all laughing. We were all drunk on cheap wine and Strongbow cider and didn't give a shit about anyone. Turned out, he was out hunting for me. Did he think he was going to beat me up this time? No chance. We were ready for him. There were about eight of us and willing to take them on, and we had all sorts of stones at our feet.

I shouted to him, "Fuck off, I'm not living in your shit house wi aw yer weans (kids). And you're not putting a finger on me or we will do the two of you, and yer car, so fuck off."

They did.

That night, or early next morning, we sneaked back into Rab's house. I now had the top bunk to myself. I was drunk, hungry and smelling of smoke from the fire we lit up on the railway bridge. I fell asleep and the next thing, the light goes on. I felt the cover getting pulled off me and a crazy-looking guy was staring at me.

"Who are you?" he asked.

"I'm Rab's pal. He said I could stay."

He dragged me out of bed. "Get out of here, you lying shit. Rab's no here."

Wee Joe was hiding under the covers. It was his da.

I got tossed out, frozen. It was about 6 in the morning and I'd nowhere to go… other than back to the house I escaped from originally. I found a shed, crumbled up in a ball and fell asleep.

I woke up and it was light. I went round to jealous Ronnie's house and asked to use his phone.

His ma got up and looked at me and said, "Where have you been, Jim? You're a mess and smelling. Go in and have a shower."

I'd never had a shower in a house before, but they had everything before anyone else had. That's why I could never understand why Ronnie was always jealous of me.

Anyway, he was ordered to give me some clothes. Alice made me a sandwich and sausage and cup of tea.

119

"Right, tell me what's happened."

I told her.

She said, "Right, do you want to phone your ma or will I do it? You need to go home, it's not right."

I said, "Can I do it?" So, I phoned my ma.

She was crying on the phone asking what's happening to me. I was crying too.

I shouted, "You and him have made me what I am. It's you two to blame. I hate both of you for it. I'm always on my own. Ever since I was ten years old you put the weight of the whole world on me. Fucking one kid after another, you getting drunk and staying out, him beating me up, his miserable misfit family hating me, you not supporting me. We are always poor. I've had to steal to support us. I've always been embarrassed by my clothes. I lost my school chance. Every day at school I was abused and laughed at…"

It all came out. I was breaking my heart.

Alice took me away. She said, "My God, son. I never knew things were that bad." Then she slapped jealous Ronnie on the head. "Why didn't you say to me? Why are you staying in Camlachie with these idiots, Jim? Why didn't you come here?"

She didn't know jealous Ronnie was hanging out in Camlachie too, but this was soon to change. By now, nothing mattered. I'd lost the will to reason or fight. At fourteen years old, I wanted to end it all, but Alice was the first comforting hand I'd felt on me for a long time. Part of my problem was I didn't tell many people about my life, only wee parts of it, then I would smile and just move on. But now I had no smile. A deal was done. Alice told me to go home and talk to my ma.

Jealous Ronnie said, "Look, there's a football game at Motherwell today. You go home, ask yer ma for the money and we can go on a supporters' bus with Ma, Da and my brothers-in-law."

I went back and spoke to Ma. She was okay. He never said anything.

Once we settled down, I said, "Ma, can I have ten bob (50p) to go to the game?"

She said, "Jim, I'm sorry, but we're skint. Yer da has lost all the money on the horses."

I just went to bed and cried. Again, nothing had changed. It was back to the way it all started. Four kids under me. He was working, but blowing the money on horses and sweets. Well, to hell with all of them. I was on my own, but I was changing. I was going to survive. I would get there. I was nearing leaving school and I couldn't wait.

Jealous Ronnie had left school by now and started working in a brewery suppliers in the East End. I knew within my heart I could have screwed my head on and stayed at school and done O levels and done something good. But after years of abuse and embarrassment due to being poor, I'd had enough. To hell with school. I was going to work anywhere that would employ me. And pay me…

My big pal Martin also got a job. He was a year older too. He got an apprentice jeweller job in a pawnshop. Not the one I pawned the nicked stuff in. He was really into it. I would go up and sit in his room the odd night and read his books on how watches and stuff worked, like what jewels in a watch did. A jewel was actually a part of the movement mechanism. *Amazing,* I thought, *maybe I could start collecting old watches and strip the jewels out of them.* But no, it wasn't that easy. I was kind of getting back into Big Martin's company. I thought, *He's a good guy. I can stay out of trouble with Big Martin...*

One night, we were looking at Big Martin's books and playing some music. He asked if I wanted to go for a bag of chips.

I said, "I've no money, Martin."

He replied, "Yeah, I've only got four bob." That was just enough to buy a bag. Then he said, "Aw, I'm getting tired. Am not gonny bother with chips."

I said, "Okay. I'm going home to let you get to bed since you have work in the morning."

Off I went. Now I only lived across the road from him. I went home and sat in my darkened room as the siblings were all asleep. I was sitting looking out of the window and there was the big fucker, rushing home with a big parcel and a bottle of Irn-Bru. I thought, *You big shite.*

I knew the girl who worked the chippy, so I climbed out my window, nipped round to there and asked her, "What did Big Martin get from here?"

She said, "Oh aye, he got a fish supper and a bottle of Irn-Bru."

Why did he do that to me? We were supposed to be pals. He knew the hardships I endured. He knew I would be starving. Next time I saw him, I told him. End of that friendship.

After that, I said to hell with this. Back to Camlachie with the gang. I got into trouble, but I trusted the idiots I was kicking about with and getting into trouble with. If two of you were screwing a shop, one got caught and one got away. No way would they grass on you. If they did, they'd get bashed up and tossed out of the gang for being a grass. Not good for the street cred. And if someone was skint, others would make sure you had food or bevvy (booze).

CHAPTER FIFTEEN

I started to have a fascination with cars. Kicking about with older guys, you pick up their habits. There was heavy talk of Fedaro Farley having his eye on a car he was going to nick.

Now this is weird. The night Rab's girl stabbed the fan to death, I usually was with them when we were mugging, but this night I had to see wee Toupence, my wee auntie. She wasn't well.

Now, on that day I did a bit of work for a shoe repairer. Big Joe the Thumb we called him. He had a cobbler business in the East End and now and then he would get me to take shoes to get the soles stitched on by another cobbler who had the machine to do it. So, he would give me the bus fare and I would carry a bag of shoes to get stitched, then go back and get them the next day. I would get a few bob and Joe always bought me a pie and peas with vinegar. I loved it and still do to this day. And also,

I would keep the bus fare and just run to the cobblers, about a twenty-minute run. Easy.

Sometimes, if my timing was right, the big rubbish truck (the clenny truck) would be heading that way and I would run and catch a niggy, which meant you ran after it and stood on the wee steps on it at the back for a free ride to wherever it was going. The driver couldn't see you. One time I got it, but I dropped the bag of shoes and they were all over the road. I had to jump off and gather them all and avoid the cars behind it all tooting horns and me giving them two fingers. Then I had to run like shit to catch the cobbler.

Now, Big Joe the Thumb was named so because he did almost everything by hand, like gluing soles and hammering tacks into heels and things. He was right-handed and his left hand was battered to bits with hammering and missing the tiny tacks, especially his thumb. It was black and about two inches wide with constantly getting hammered. Hence the title. He was a big guy. Dead ringer for Shrek from the movie, ugly as a demon, but a really nice generous big guy. Always whistling, except when he hit his thumb.

So, I was on my way with the sack of shoes, thinking about my upcoming meal of a hot pie and peas and vinegar from the wee shop next door to Joe's shop. It was another day when not much was in the house to eat, so this pie was important. I'd got the run done and back and munched my five-star dining and now was heading back to Camlachie. It was just after shop closing time and still light. Back then, all the shops closed at 5 p.m., not a minute later. You could not buy a loaf of bread or milk or anything the grocers sold. After that, it was chip shops and pubs that were open.

In 1970, a wee Pakistani guy called George and his Scottish wife Elsie opened a shop, a grocer's shop. First in the area. He opened from 10 a.m. to 10 p.m. It was amazing. You could go get bread, milk, fags, anything. All the shops were shitting themselves and he was a smashing wee guy. If you were a few coppers short and he knew you, you could pay later. He started the "tick book", which, to those privileged few who didn't experience it, was a credit book. You paid him on the Friday. Of course, many didn't and didn't get back in the shop.

When I was on my way to meet the gang, I walked along past the graveyard wall of Janefield Street, which connects Springy Road to Holywell Street, where the Cardowan Creamery is and still is on a lesser scale, and past the Camlachie Cooperage where they made the barrels for sherry and whisky.

One night, we broke in there. We burst some of the barrels that were sweating the alcohol, which meant if they had been holding whisky for a long time the wood absorbed some of it in the process. Maybe like the "angel share", so they sat there to sweat and the white wood alcohol would lie at the bottom of the barrels. Our task was to whack the arse of the barrels, without making a noise, and drain the fluid via a funnel into ginger bottles. Small bits of wood and all. We knew a few alcoholics who would buy them from us. One being the chip shop guy, so he would give us chips as well as payment and get pissed out his head for days. God help the chips.

Anyway, I was heading towards the railway arches and I could see a few guys hanging about. I had to be careful in case they were the Spur gang. Once you went through the arch, it opened up to the sprawling estate of

Barrowfield Street, Camlachie. A very dark and dangerous place if you were a stranger… of any age. A pure shithouse by description and a lot of weird filthy inbred ugly kids waiting to mug you.

I asked one of the guys what was going on. He said Fedaro had nicked a car. They were going mental up and down the streets and screaming around corners. I could hear it coming. A big yellow Morris 1700, powerful car.

They approached at a very high speed. Fedaro was driving with jealous Ronnie in the front passenger and two guys in the back seat (one of which I knew as Whitey). I knew it wasn't right, too fast. They were all waving and shouting. He took a very sharp bend too fast, bounced off the side wall of the arch and swung to the right. A head-on full pelt into a wall. Jealous Ronnie went right through the windscreen and over the bonnet. Fedaro was jammed against the steering wheel. Whitey was almost decapitated and dead. The other guy was badly injured. All in two minutes.

There was silence, then blind panic. The car was smoking. I ran and grabbed Ronnie, dragging him away. He was semi-conscious and bleeding very badly. He was

129

always a heavily built young guy. I managed to lift him over my shoulder and I dragged him away towards his house. All the way I was talking to him and trying to make up a story for his ma. He lived about 300 yards away around the corner. I made it to his close and sat him down.

"Look, Ronnie," I said, "We were playing football and you ran down a hill to get the ball and ran into rusty railings at full speed."

He was bleeding heavily. It was all over me. I could smell it. For the first time since I'd known him since six years old, I really felt sorry for him and I thought he was going to die.

I dragged him up to his top floor house and banged the door. His sister opened it and started screaming in horror. That brought his ma and Steve McQueer the brother who took it up the boys' gate in the nick. He stood there white-faced.

I shouted, "Give me a hand."

We got him into the kitchen and his sister phoned 999 immediately. Before asking what happened, his wee ma was crying and all upset. I told her our made-up story. She listened but never really reasoned with it. We cleaned him up a bit, but blood was pouring out of him. Now he was feeling the pains. Then his ma pulled pieces of glass from him.

"What's this?"

I said in panic, "He fell on glass too."

She looked at me and said, "Jim, if you're lying, I'll fucking kill you."

Just then, the ambulance arrived for him. By now, the word was on the street and cops were everywhere. The ambulance man told his ma he was likely a victim of the car crash and would inform police by radio.

We got him to hospital. I couldn't go, so when they left, I nipped back round to the scene of horrors. The car was mangled and had a lot of blood in it. An ambulance and two cop cars were still there. Turned out, Whitey was dead in the ambulance. So sad. He was sixteen. Only son of a single parent.

Back at the infirmary, I found out they removed a dozen pieces of glass from Ronnie's face alone. He broke his nose and had other minor injuries. Fedaro, the crazy driver, escaped with a broken arm and scratches. The other guy had major injuries. I never knew who that guy was. Thing is, if I hadn't been going to the cobblers, I would have been in that car. So, being skint and hungry and the wish for the pie and peas possibly saved my life. Somebody up there must have liked me, but who?

Jealous Ronnie got out of hospital. His ma and sisters, and now his wee da Pat, were all pissed off. They wanted to know why he was there, why he was with the guys involved, and why I never told them. Me? My fault again.

I just said, "Ask him, he can tell you."

So, he did. And I decided then that I should stay back from there. I'd had two near misses, with the stabbing and now this. It could be third time unlucky.

Wee Rab got three months in the nick. He was my pal. His bird Ann got life. So, things were not the same, but there was a court case to come up. A young guy died. Fedaro was in custody as the taker of the car and responsible as the driver. Whitey had an uncle who was notorious in the East End. A guy who would do you without conscience, and the word was out: Fedaro was a target. And he was shitting himself…

CHAPTER SIXTEEN

I met Big Martin again. Jealous Ronnie was badly scarred and kept indoors. His face was a mess. His hair was shaved due to the cuts he obtained. So, he was out of the equation. My fifteenth birthday was coming up and I was looking for a job. I was due to leave school at the summer, but I would turn fifteen on May 7th, so if I could get my national insurance number by then, I could start work before I left in June.

Big Martin got sacked from the pawn for stealing jewellery and he got a job beside jealous Ronnie in the beer suppliers in Bridgeton.

He said, "If you get your number, I'll get you a start in with us."

Well, with Ronnie off work, I had to rely on Martin.

I went to my ma and asked where my birth certificate was. Now, Weird Da Jim never liked me. His family hated me. His old ma would come to our house and I was told to call her Nana. I fucking refused point blank and through the years took a few slaps for it, but she wasn't my nana. If she was, I still wouldn't call her nana. She didn't like me. She focused on the others who were his. I knew all this, but didn't understand it.

My ma said, "I haven't got your birth certificate."

I said, "Okay, where do I get it?"

She said, "Martha Street registry office in town."

So, me and Big Martin headed into Martha Street, waited in the queue and asked the woman for what I needed.

She said, "You're too young. I need a letter from your mother."

So, we headed back.

The next day, I said, "Hey, Ma. They need a note."

So, she wrote a note and we headed into town. We were in the cubicle, laughing away as you do at fifteen. The woman took the note, went away for a bit, then came back.

As bold as you like, she said, "Look, son. Your birth certificate is in Edinburgh. You're adopted."

Well, I fell on my arse. So did Martin. Back then, if you were different, you were spoken about. And I was different. But everything that I had experienced all fell into place. Now I knew why the family hated me, why I got the beatings, why old fucking Nana never liked me. I felt relieved, but why did my ma never back me up, and where was my real da, Pat, and the Addams family who showed me so much love. Answers I would find later...

She sent me away to ask my mother. Quite hard but that's the way it was then. So, I questioned my ma, who never gave much away.

I said, "Okay, I'll write to Edinburgh."

So, I had to wait weeks for the birth certificate to come through, but I got it. I didn't care about the circumstances. I wanted to work, so I never asked any questions and never got any answers...

I returned to wee Toupence and my uncle and asked them, but they were not for giving much away. Until they had a drink in them. So, I waited till a Friday night when they had a drink. They spilled the beans about my real da and what had happened. Turned out, when my uncle

137

was in Borstal, my ma fell for Da Pat when they both were fifteen. They were inseparable, in love.

Now, as my ma was the youngest sister, the others left the home and she was left alone to look after her ma and da. It became obvious my real da Pat was a threat, so they set upon turning my ma against him. My ma fell pregnant and Real Da Pat was all excited, even though back then this was a bad thing. He set upon getting a house and getting married as it was the respectable thing to do and they loved each other. But my ma had been brainwashed and didn't want to see him. Very cruel.

My uncle got out of Borstal, so he looked after my ma when she was near to giving birth to me. Real Da Pat was broken-hearted as my ma would not let him see me. So, I took my uncle's surname as a middle name with no father on the birth certificate, and my surname was my ma's surname.

My uncle married wee Toupence and they were to be my godparents. My real da tried his best to get my ma, but she was too far compromised by her quite ill parents. She could not leave them, although she was mad in love with Real Da Pat, so a sacrifice was made. Me... as usual.

My ma brought me up. Toupence was always near at hand, but fair play to my ma, she always kept in touch with Real Da Pat's mum, aka Mrs McDunoch, and Auntie Rose with the funny eyes. I never knew his dad. My real grandad.

So, that's why I had the pram journeys till I was almost five years old. Real Da Pat got so fed up with my ma, he met someone else and made way to Canada. My ma had met Weird Da Jim and I was left behind at four years old without my father. But it wasn't his fault. We were all victims of circumstance, but at the time I didn't know. Once he was gone out of the scene, the visits stopped. I think my ma was heart-broken, but she never ever said. I know now she made the wrong decision, but hindsight is great, as you will learn later in my story.

Now I was about to venture into the world with a new so-called father I didn't know and a family who hated me.

I got the job in the beer place and I was delighted. I got the job in the loading bay. I wanted the van boy job, but it didn't really matter. I soon learnt how to drive the fork truck and the routine and stock control. Jealous Ronnie started back. He worked in the loading bay also, a floor below me. He saw I was doing really well and, again, turned against me, but it never really bothered me. I focused on earning money. Now, he was also well in with a big security guy who was ruthless in his ways, always wanting to catch guys on the fiddle. I was well aware of him.

I started to work out how to make some extra cash on the side. I knew this job was temporary as I wanted to work with cars. Use the brains I was born with. Brains I used to get to a good school.

Before long, I was throwing out cases of beer to a select few drivers who in turn would give me payment on their return. I was cashing in big time, but I made two mistakes. First, I got greedy. Second, I never took into account that Ronnie's wee brother-in-law was a driver and was a grass to the security. Even though I had heard about him, I underestimated him. So, one of the drivers I was giving a turn to mentioned it to him. He told Ronnie who in turn told the security guy. Well, that's how I assumed it went.

My ma was back to being always skint, kids hungry, Weird Da Jim not working. Same old, same old, now with more mouths to feed.

I earnt £3 a week. I had £20 in my pocket on a Wednesday night due to my fiddle. I would give my ma half of what I had. She would not ask where I got it. I was earning more than he did, if he worked.

I knew my time was coming. The security was after me, but by now I was going to start an apprenticeship as a mechanic, so I didn't give a shit. Also, I was heavy drinking on a Friday night and Saturday night as I had the money to do so.

One Friday after work, we all got into the pubs. I was on the whisky. I had bought my wee brother a ball for his birthday and gave it to him on the Friday night. I was pissed out of my head.

I said, "Here's a ball for yer birthday. Don't say about me being drunk."

What did he do? Ran straight home and told Weird Da Jim who, by now, I didn't give a shit about and didn't fear him, but he was after payback on me. So, knowing Auntie Jean was coming on the Saturday, he told her.

141

Now, she was not just violent, but also an alcoholic by this time, and now even I was afraid of her.

I got up on the Saturday, hungover but not caring. I just wanted to get back out there. That's when I found out what had been said. I met my ma and Auntie Jean on the street. Bang! Auntie Jean whacked me.

I asked, "What was that for?"

She said, "You were drunk last night. He told me, you fucking idiot. Your brother shopped you."

I said, "I'm sorry, Auntie Jean. It was my pals who made me do it."

She said, "I'm not caring who made you do it. I don't care if you got drunk. I know you've been good to your ma."

I asked, "Why did you hit me then?"

She said, "Because you got caught and gave that bastard reason to come and tell me. Next time, don't get caught. In fact, whatever you get up to in life, if you get caught, don't blame anybody but yourself because if they don't know, they can't shop you."

That has stuck with me all my life.

I went straight home and put a knife into the little fucker's new ball. *Go tell yer da now...* It was his last birthday present from me.

I started playing cards and gambling on the horses in the bookies called John Banks. You had to be eighteen, but I always got served, due to being popular and everyone knowing me in my errand days.

I first got served at fourteen years old. My ma sent me to put on a horse on the Grand National. I loved the buzz in the bookies and was addicted to it. Back then, a wee man was on a stage who listened to commentaries on a speaker and marked the betting on the boards. That year, her horse won. It was called "Gay Trip" with the oldest jockey called Pat Taaffe at forty years old. Can you imagine a horse called that now...?

It was a happy day that day as Weird Da Jim had it on also. We all had a wedding to go to that night and it meant there was money in the pot to carry us. We took an old auntie called Lizzy also. She had no teeth and didn't give a shit. All her four sons were in jail, so she had nobody except us. I didn't really know her very well, other than her sons were notorious in the East End. My cousins.

Back then, you just wrote the horse and the race on any old bit of paper or on the back of a cigarette packet. You identified yourself by a "nom de plume" on the paper, which was anything or code relating to you only, along with your bet. So, if you had a winner, you went up to get your money by giving your nom de plume. Mine was "Jim 14", first name and age I first got served. I later obtained my first private registration for my car when I was forty-five years old, and that's what it was: JM 14. Cost me £250...

Saying I was getting greedy in the loading bay was an understatement. I was now putting out full pallets of beer, i.e. forty cases at a time. I got £20 for each pallet. In one day, I slung out three pallets. I didn't give a hoot as I was leaving in a couple of weeks. It was easy and quick as I was now trusted to drive the fork truck and full load the trucks for the heavier runs. The drivers had the load checkers in their pocket, so everyone got paid for the turn. But the security man was closing in.

I heard again jealous Ronnie had grassed on me, so it ended on the Friday night. I left that night later to find out that the security had planned to trap me on the Monday. Third time lucky in my young life. The stabbing, the crash and now this. How far could I push my luck?

CHAPTER SEVENTEEN

I was almost sixteen and wanted an apprenticeship. I wanted to work on cars. Or at least, I wanted to drive them, ASAP. Weird Da Jim had a job in a factory producing meats, pies and stuff to supply shops and, most of all, the hundreds of fish and chip shops we had all around Scotland, and especially Glasgow, at that time. I had no job, so that meant he had to keep me and he didn't like it, even though I'd kept him by stealing in the past. This company had a big fleet of about twenty vans, all makes and sizes, so he spoke for me to get a start. I was offered and accepted.

Glasgow was big on chip shops, all Italian, as we got a big intake of Italians in the south and east of Glasgow from the thirties, forties and fifties. Most of them made good opening up ice cream cafes and chip shops. To this day, they are the best. I would never buy fish and chips or any supper, and the pickles have to be Gold Star, from a chip shop that isn't Italian. But nowadays, they are few and far between. The younger brigade now are into other things like pakoras, pizzas, burger bars and all continental type junk food made easier by technology.

We had Tony Capaldi's, Ronnie Connetta's and his mother Lucy Connetta, Coronation Cafe, Coia's, Enzo's, Salvadori's… the best chippies in the city, and many more I can't remember the names of, but all good nosh. Back in the day, you could not beat a bag of chips on a cold night soaked in salt, vinegar and brown sauce. If you were trying to impress a female, it was a fish supper between you.

I started my first day and there were three old-looking guys: one good, one always drunk and the oldest, Johnny, who never knew what day of the week it was. He never spoke to me much at all. Also, there was an older apprentice called Henny. Big guy, quiet, but well respected and clever.

So, that was me in. I was dying to get tore in and learn the game, but I wanted to drive the vans even more. My wage was £3 again, and I was getting sent to college on day release. Apart from the garage, there was the main factory also. The drunk guy, Wattie, was very clever. He could turn his hand to most things. Ex-RAF engineer, so he was the foreman mechanic and factory maintenance man. The good old guy Alec, he just stuck to the mechanics, but he had a very short temper and was always shouting and bawling.

After a few weeks, I was getting settled in, but it was a 7 a.m. start till 5 p.m. finish. A lot for a sixteen-year-old kicking about till midnight hour during the week, waiting on a Friday to party, drinking in the pub in Parkhead, The Black Bull. Then Friday night was Barrowland night. Saturday night was cheap carry out night, or to the pictures if you had a bird (female companion) and a cheap carry out. Then back to being skint the rest of week, but who cared if you had a great weekend.

Before my sixteenth birthday, I had two made-to-measure suits. Dapper I was. One from John Temple and one from Jackson's. Both top tailors in their day. You went and got measured up, paid the suit price over six weeks and it was ready. I used my extra wages from the beer factory to buy them. I also had a pair of Terry's shoes and a pair of Chelsea boots. All top "in vogue" kit.

I swore to myself at fifteen nobody would ever take me down again for my clothes. I've continued that through my life and onto my kids. At over sixty now, I still keep up with the style, to a certain degree, but always smart, casual or dress (still go to Dee's of Trongate and TK Maxx, best shops ever for clothes). You should always take pride in yourself, no matter how up in years you are. There is always someone noticing what you're wearing. Younger ones are always curious about your style. Older ones are always jealous they never had the balls to buy what you're wearing and let themselves go.

It may sound weird that at sixteen I would want to wear a made-to-measure suit, but that was the style then. We all wore them. At least, most of us did. All smart. And secondly, you learnt how to dance. Both assets in the "Georgie's Byre". Look "byre" up in the dictionary and you will know what I mean. The byre was downstairs in the Barrowland all dimly lit with cubicles and big sofas.

Back to Monday. I was told I had to attend day release the next day and every Tuesday. It was away over in Langside, two bus journeys away. I was always skint on a Tuesday. I was always skint on the Sunday! I didn't have my "extra" earnings I was getting before and I was finding it very difficult to get by.

Big Henny the other apprentice had been teaching me how to shunt the vans in and out and I was loving driving, even though I was only in first gear most of the time. He started telling me about a wee bit of business he was into to earn a bit on the side. Now I was interested as I was down to one suit as a bird I took to the Olympia picture house one Saturday night in Bridgeton lit a cigarette and bumped it against my leg burning a hole on the thigh of my favourite petrol blue Jackson's suit. I loved that suit. Now, at J3 per week, I couldn't buy another. I was raging at her.

Big Henny started telling me about the turn. A guy he knew had a car business. By now, I was picking up things very good and learning the tools. Henny had noticed this too. The deal was, it was parts to order. Back then, there was no CCTV, so what we did was go out at night in Henny's car and go round the car dealers who had cars lying in open yards, mostly in the posh areas like Uddingston, Bothwell, Bearsden and Newton Mearns. If we needed a front bumper for a Ford Cortina or fancy wheels for a Jag or whatever it was, we would scan around for the car we wanted, go at night with the tools and start stripping off the bumper from a Cortina on show. If we needed a door or boot lid, it was more money for us. Sports car stuff was expensive. We then moved up to stealing a full car. We did it once, got chased by cops, but got away after we dumped the car. So, for a wee while, we were doing okay.

Henny had a brother who was also in on the scam with us. I was working away by day, learning what I could, and I'd also started showing interest in maintenance in the factory with Wattie the drunk genius. Now I was fixing hoovers and things for workers. Word gets about fast when you're handy. I loved it. Doing it during work hours was even better. Only thing was, I couldn't be arsed with college, so I wasn't attending. To be honest, my days at St Mungo's scarred me for life regarding classroom stuff. To this day, I don't like it.

One day, I was at college and Big Henny came to pick me up in a white Jaguar S type triple X model. Beautiful it was. He had just bought it. I thought, *I want a car like this. When I pass my test.*

After that, I lost interest in college. I was doing my thing during the week, helping Henny with the cars at night when required, and partying at weekends. I'd also met a girl, so my time was occupied. Also, I was betting on the horses and losing money as fast as I was earning it.

My ma had accepted a house exchange to a place way out near Easterhouse, which had the reputation of Apache territory, which devastated me. Another thing I held against her all my life, just like when she left me to be so scared in the house with the kids while she was out flirting till all hours. She never ever told me she loved me. I never ever told her. It has a drastic effect on a kid through to adult, like you're left in limbo. You never get an explanation.

I hated it at the new house. Each night, if I got off the bus, I would get chased by local thugs who never knew me. I took a kicking one night from four of them. After that, they didn't bother me. I still hated the place. Later in life, I was to share a bit of smoking dope and card games with the same gang members. Life can be weird. For later chapters…

153

Big Henny would come pick me up some nights we had a wee job on. My ma didn't like him and Weird Da Jim knew him from working in the same place. He knew what was going on, but didn't show any interest. Meanwhile, I was still kicking about with jealous Ronnie, but the Camlachie crowd were out of my life after the crash. Ronnie had terrible facial scars and a bent beak due to trying to fly while in a stolen car. Fedaro got three months in the nick. When he got out, he couldn't live with the fact a guy got killed. He became a homeless alcoholic and died aged twenty-two.

Ronnie was back to his confident self and jealous I had an apprenticeship. Big Martin and him were still in the beer factory and he was still a nice big guy even though he done me for a fish supper. I got over that. He later became an alcoholic after getting jilted by a girl called Mary who he was mad about. He died at thirty-eight. Very sad. I met his younger brother some years later. He was on heroin. Who knows where he is now…

I'd got rid of the girl I was with. Too busy in my life to be tied down. And too skint.

One Saturday morning, Henny came to get me. He had a plan to make money. Celtic and Rangers were playing at Ibrox. Big turnout. The plan was we would go in a stolen white Triumph which was stashed. We'd take a bunch of keys each and take a street of cars each and take what we could from them and sell it off.

So, me, him and his brother Rusty set off in the afternoon in the stolen car. It was parked at Dumbreck Road. We set off armed with keys, pliers and small screwdrivers, ready to take radios and 8-track cassette players. Anything else worth taking, we took and kept taking it back to the Triumph and then back to the cars.

After a bit of time, we had to be away before the game came out. We had arranged to meet at the Triumph, which wasn't locked and get out of there with the gear. We all got into the car and it was packed with coats, jackets, radios, everything we stole. Just as we took off, police appeared from all angles. Big Henny was a good driver. This was the second cop chase we'd had and he got us away the first time as I said earlier. I was buzzing and confident and hoping he'd get away, but the cops were on our tail. They were driving wee crap Ford Anglias. We had a big Triumph. No contest.

As soon as we had a clear way, Henny shouted, "Get out and run."

We did and parted. The Triumph smacked a wall with all doors open. I had a navy jumper on with a T-shirt under it. It was mid-October and was very dry and cold. I jumped down a railway embankment and hid in the bushes for what seemed like hours. I lay and heard all the cars on the main road. I knew that was the game coming out, so I waited until it got quieter. I removed my jumper and headed out to the road. It was getting a bit dark and I wasn't sure which direction I was heading. A police panda car passed me and ahead of me was this big guy with bushy hair walking. I looked back and saw the panda doing a U-turn. I was in trouble. I couldn't run, so I joined the big guy and walked alongside him.

I said, "Look, big man. Cops are after me. I'm just walking with you till they pass."

But they didn't. They stopped and pulled us both.

I said, "Me and my mate are just walking along the road."

The cop said, "What's his name?" Damn it. "And also, why are you just wearing a T-shirt on a cold day?" Double damn it.

I was fucked. They piled us in to the cop car in the back seat. The big guy was crying and telling them what happened. During this, I still had the bunch of car keys in my pocket. I forgot to dump them, so I was looking at the cop in his mirror and I was slowly tucking the keys down the back of the seat. Success, I thought, but as the car turned a corner the keys start rattling against the metal under the seat. I saw the cop's eyes on me in the mirror. Triple damn it. He knew.

We got to Govan cop shop and it was noisy with drunken fans. I got questioned about who I was with, but my days running about Camlachie reminded me to not grass on anyone. I didn't and they weren't happy, but what I didn't know was they already had Henny's brother in as they caught him. A man and woman saw him doing the cars and followed him. They took note of the cars while they waited on the cops as they had phoned them.

I got taken to the cells upstairs. My first experience of jail. As we approached the cell, all these shoes were lying outside, loads of them. The cop opened the cell and there were bodies everywhere. It stunk. Twelve in total. I was lucky thirteen. I thought at last my luck had run out.

Due to the football, there were massive arrests back then for drinking and fighting. Old firm matches were the same to this day, although CCTV has stemmed it inside grounds.

Next day, Sunday, I was shipped to Pollack cop station. It was about 6 p.m. and I was starving. The cops had been to my house and informed the parents. My ma had stuck Big Henny in the shit, giving his name and where he worked and how he picked me up on the Saturday. Now I was worried he would think I'd grassed on him. Tactic the cops used.

I'll never forget the turnkey guy. He was a real decent guy. He brought me in a pie supper from the nearby chippy. It made a real bad day all of a sudden a real good day.

✦ ✦ ✦

On the Monday morning, myself and a few others were handcuffed and taken to Barlinnie dog boxes as they were known. Four of you in one but only two could sit down. It was about 6 a.m. Then we got driven to the old central court in town. I appeared in front of a judge and was told to appear in late November. Thank God I was away from there. Freedommmm!

Big Henny got arrested on the Monday and appeared the next day. He got the same date as me and his brother to appear.

In this time, Weird Da Jim had bought a Ford Cortina, a green one. I was back at work and me and Henny were doing a bit of work on it. I bought chrome wheels from a guy I knew and we put a 1500cc engine in it. It looked the part. So, because I did the work, I was able to drive about in it, even though I had no licence as I was too young.

Through a girl Henny was seeing, I'd got a blind date with her pal. We met up at Bothwell Hotel. I'd got the Cortina. She was a bit on the ugly side, but we all got pissed anyway. Henny went his way and we went in my car. I was driving in Bothwell, a place I didn't know, and I was drunk with a girl I didn't know and who was at

159

my rear? The cops. I took the first available left then the blue light came on. It was a one way and I was facing it. Huckled again.

We were taken back to Uddingston cop shop. The girl was crying as she lived miles away. They let her out and I never saw her again. I never understood why. We got on so well…

I got charged with drunk driving, no licence or insurance and taking a car without consent. I got bailed to appear at a later date. I got let out about 7 a.m. and had to walk home to Barlanark. Took hours. Then I had to tell Weird Da Jim I got lifted and they had his car in the softest voice I could as I woke him up from a sleep, just like when I escaped from Auntie Georgie's. Only he had different underpants on, but the same stinking socks.

When I got over the "Good morning, Daddy, how are you today?" bit, I said, "I've been in the nick all night. They have your car."

I walked past him and went to my bed. Now, had it been three or four years earlier, I would have been dead for sure. At the very worst, made to wear his pants and socks for a day.

He followed me into the room I shared with my brother without a ball.

"What do you mean they have the car?"

"Well, I've no licence, and you knew I had the car, so it's your fault."

Now he was shouting at me.

I said, "Oh, aye, I was drunk too. So, I'm on a charge."

He turned and stormed out the room. I looked at him, noticing his baggy underpants had a big brown streak on the arse part. I started laughing. I was still half drunk.

He stormed back into the room, fist in the air as if he was ready to lay into me.

I got up and shouted, "Don't you fucking touch me or I swear I'll stab you in your sleep. I'm not afraid of you."

He eased off, rage in his eyes and started leaving the room.

I shouted, "Go wash yer pants." Ha ha ha, made my morning.

On the Sunday afternoon, his pal ran us over to Uddingston cop shop to get the car. I admitted to taking it without his consent to save his arse.

The cop said, "Before you get the car, the handbrake isn't holding, so it's not roadworthy."

I always had tools in the boot, so I had to lie in the rain in the yard under the car and tighten the handbrake cable. Weird Da Jim had that look in his eyes as I lay there. Payback.

After that, I ceased all bad activity. I had two major charges coming up and I wasn't seventeen yet. I started to realise what a mess I was making of my life, and also knew my luck had run out.

Our court date arrived for late November for the car theft and stealing from cars. It was a bad one because some fans drove from far and wide for the game and had to come back here for the court and to claim what they lost. I felt so bad for them and sorry for what I did.

CHAPTER EIGHTEEN

I was now seventeen. Court was near and I was shitting myself. On the day we were there, a wee court lawyer we had said to plead guilty and we would likely get a fine. We did and got twenty-eight days remand for background reports rammed up our arses.

I was in shock. Prison? I'd never been in prison. Why? We never harmed anybody. What I didn't know was Rusty had many previous, so that affected us. We got sent down to the holding cells of the central court. I didn't even know where I was going to be.

We eventually got called and got handcuffed to each other, maybe about a dozen of us. I was attached to a skinhead type guy, only later to realise he had lice. And if you had them, your hair got shaved and deloused.

We were in the paddy wagon on the way to Longriggend remand prison. I was half excited and half afraid.

It looked like I was the youngest-looking amongst us. Although I was seventeen, I didn't look it.

It was about 6 p.m. when we got there. A guy asked me if I'd been in before.

I said, "No, first time."

He asked what age I was.

I said, "Seventeen."

He said, "That's good as you will get a pint with your dinner at night."

Wow, I thought, *can't be that bad.* And since I'd been drinking in pubs at fourteen, it didn't worry me about the pint. I could handle that.

We entered Longriggend. It was a dark and dreary place. It was for young offenders awaiting trial or, for some, awaiting bail or fines being paid. I got escorted by the screws to the bar (not the pints bar), got signed in and I was put in a cell by myself. I could hear howling and shouting and banging, like being in a zoo for humans.

I was sitting in the wee cell and it was very cold. There was a coal shortage that time (it was November 1973), so the prison had no heating. I wrapped the bed blankets around me to keep warm. I looked out of the window and it was bleak and dark. I had no idea where it was, but there was nothing but darkness.

The cell door opened.

The screw said, "You've got a visitor. Special privilege."

He escorted me to a room where inside was wee Auntie Toupence, heavily pregnant. I got a shock, but was relieved to see her. I gave her a hug before realising she was really here.

"What the hell you doing here at this hour?"

She said, "I came to see you. You can't sit here alone."

I said, "You're pregnant. What are you doing?"

That's the way she was. She would help anyone. Turned out, when she found out about me, she was at court and I didn't know. She asked where I was going and made her own way to get to the prison. She got a lift to Airdrie, then walked to the prison, which was a couple of miles away, in the dark and pregnant. It was too late for buses as they only ran for visiting times, but the prison officer, seeing what she had done to get to me, let her see me briefly then offered to run her back home to the East End. Luckily, the car was going back to Barlinnie which was in the East End. She was happy about that and seeing me. Bless her wee soul. She went on to give birth to a boy, John, who is my godson.

Next morning, it was bang bang at the doors. It was 6 a.m. All out for a shower and breakfast. My first morning on what felt like death row. I got a ten-second shower, then down for a mug of tea and porridge and a roll. Then we were escorted to the medical block for inspection by hand lamp. We all stripped off completely. We stood in a row, went into a line up and waited to be inspected by supposed doctors.

"Stand in front, turn around, face the wall, bend over forwards."

Then he held an inspection lamp, like the one in the garage I used, and had a peep up your arsehole. What he was looking for, I had no idea, but I knew I didn't have it. Then it was a lamp on your head looking for lice and other creepy crawlies you may find. Now, I had a good long head of hair and I was shitting it thinking they would chop it, but they didn't. Thank God. Some were not so lucky. These guys were not hairdressers. It was blunt clippers all around your head then a talcum puffed over you for nits and lice if you had them. All they needed was a striped suit and they fitted the bill for a movie. Not for me.

We then got took for uniforms and registration of the crime committed. They asked what you were in for, even though they knew, and you had to shout out, while standing stark naked.

"Car theft," I shouted.

If you were in for anything like messing with kids or old people, you were in trouble as everyone would know and you were a target. Back then, if you did any of that shit, you got punished badly, like I did to the wee fat pervert who had a go at the wee girl in my close. No silly do-gooders protecting them like we have now. If you couldn't sort them, the local hard men did…

I was in the row waiting on my uniform: prison issue, itchy woollen tunic and trousers in a navy colour. Two shirts, blue and white striped, one pair of shoes, each a different size. Think I was a size 7 back then and one was an 8.

Now, remember Auntie Georgie trying to get my pants off for bath time? When I said they looked like the ones Jesus wore on the cross all baggy? Well, welcome to prison issue. He must have been here before. They were the same fucking pants. Had to be clipped to my nipples to hold them up. So, there I was, all suited and booted and nowhere to dance, especially with two odd-sized shoes. I must have looked like Charlie Chaplin without the cane and the hat…

Back to our cells. I'd briefly spoken to Henny and Rusty. We were all okay, but Rusty had bumped into a guy he had a run-in with outside and he was worried. Big Henny couldn't help him and I was staying out of it. I'd met a guy called Bekky who I knew from Camlachie. He'd acclimatised to the regime and knew a few guys inside, so I was okay. He was on me and watching my back.

My second night I was alone again, but I'd decided I was here for a month and I needed to stay away from the maddies, not upset anyone and get out. And stay away from lice and keep my hair.

After night time tea, we got an hour of TV before lockdown at 9 p.m. That was where everyone sized up who was who. I'd met Bekky again and we had a chat about why I was in and for how long. Because of the crimes I committed, I was an okay guy as I said before. Before lights out, I got a big chunk of fruit bread and a mug of tea. Just what you need. No Horlicks in here.

On day three, I was still looking for a correct size matching shoe as every time I tried to walk, the bigger shoe came off. I looked like I walked like Ratso from the *Midnight Cowboy* movie. Dustin Hoffman played him superb.

I was still waiting for the pint I was told about, so I caught Bekky at supper that night and asked him. He almost choked.

"You fucking idiot. Who told you that? It's a half pint you get." He looked at me and laughed again. "Where do you think you are, the Central Hotel?"

I laughed with him as if to show I knew it was a wind up. I was deeply upset about this. Idiot I was.

There were always fights going on. Scary actually. I saw a young guy get his face slashed badly, but not with a knife. The guy used a fork on him. Nasty mess it made to his face.

As I said, there was no coal about. Everywhere was shutting down. In prison, we had no heating for two weeks, so it was up at 5:30 a.m. in prison issue vest and shorts, and my two odd shoes, and down to the gym for a run about for an hour with a medicine ball. It was heavier than me. The vest and shorts were too big for me as well. I thought, *This takes me back to St Mungo's.* But this time, we were all equal. Well, nearly. Once I found a size 7 right shoe, I'd be equal. Or a size 8. Either way, they would be the same size. I was trying to run to keep warm and the bloody shoe kept falling off.

On the fourth day, I was moved to another cell. There was a young guy already there called Jugs from Saltcoats. Very nervous and prancing up and down the eight-foot-long cell.

"You're on the left side bunk," he said.

"Okay, no problem."

"Do you smoke?" he asked.

"Aye," I said, "But I've none. I've no money either."

He was frantic for a smoke. Turned out, he'd been in for three weeks waiting on someone paying his bail till he went back to court. He had no money at all. *Join the fucking gang*, I thought, *I've been like that all my life.*

After an hour prancing about, he said, "Let me see your jacket."

"What for?" I asked.

"A smoke," he said.

"What? You're gonny smoke my jacket?"

"No chance," he said, "No, let me see it."

He dug into the pockets and scraped out the shit and fluff at the bottom of each pocket where, to my surprise, there were tiny bits of tobacco amongst it all. He rolled all the shit in a fag paper and smoked it in one big toke. It went up in blue smoke burning his lips.

"Ahh, that's better. I'm calmer now."

No smoke detectors back then. I never slept that night... and I kept my jacket on.

Next day, I was moved again. I'd been in almost a week with no visit from my ma or the other half of the duo, Skiddy Pants.

This time, I was dubbed up with a guy called "Moose". He was eighteen and bald headed with a fluffy beard. He was obsessed with his teeth and constantly brushed them. Every time he spoke, he brushed his teeth. And, to be honest, I remember thinking, *This clown doesn't even have nice teeth.*

I had a visit call on the seventh day: my ma and Skiddy. My ma was all upset and crying. He said nothing at all, just sat there looking at me.

I said, "Don't worry, Ma. I'm fine."

"What about this drunk driving? You're going to be in again."

"For fuck's sake, Ma. Let me get by this one first."

"We can't keep coming here. It's too expensive."

"Okay, what's new?" I said, "Don't worry about it, I'll survive."

Away they went.

My days and nights went by without much hassle, although I got pulled out a line up one day after being in three weeks. I have a birthmark on my neck area, and the screws thought it was a love bite. No chance. Scary thought.

I never got any more visits. Wee Toupence was too near the birth of the baby and my good uncle had become a recluse.

CHAPTER NINETEEN

I got my appearance at court date. It was Boxing Day. *Weird*, I thought, *but okay for me*. I hoped…

On Christmas Eve, we got TV as usual, but a fight broke out over what channel to watch with some guys. We only had four channels. We all got sent to our peters (prison slang for cells).

At about midnight, someone started singing Jingle Bells. We had a big heating pipe that ran through the cell walls. We all gradually joined in singing then started to tap our tin mugs off of the pipe. Before we knew it, we had a rave going on. It was magic.

Next morning, Christmas Day, we all got our usual exercise, then showers, breakfast and back up to the peter. Then we got called out in rows and given a half bar each of Highland Toffee for our Christmas. Wow, this was way better than bananas.

Our highlight was Top of the Pops at 2 p.m. on BBC One. Leo Sayer or Slade were number one at the time. Bloody screws barred us due to the previous night's fiasco. Major loss. Everyone in the UK watched Tops on Christmas Day. Buggers. But we got our Christmas dinner of turkey and the works. Think that was the first time I ever had turkey and the works. Better than fucking bananas. This was the life.

Next day, Boxing Day, we were up at 6 a.m. No exercise, just a mug of tea and a roll, then on to the happy bus to the central court in town, which was about an hour away. Again, handcuffed to each other.

We got there about 9 a.m. and put into holding cells again, where you met Glasgow's best lawyers, the ex-cons waiting on trial. They could tell who's who of judges, lawyers, what your punishment would be… The real lords of the penal system. So they thought.

It was our turn after about three hours on hold. I was very nervous. I didn't want to go back in there. I'd made my mind up that when this was all over, I was done with all the stupid daft things I'd done, and I would not be back, even if it was for Christmas dinner. No more for me.

We were escorted into court from the cells below. It was horrible being so young. I deserved everything I got for the hurt I caused different people in different ways. I was ashamed of the selfishness of my ways, but in my mind, it was survival in a difficult environment and, of course, my shit upbringing. All this was going through my mind walking up the stairs handcuffed to a court officer and into the big courtroom. I remember looking to my left and a reporter was writing stuff. I remember seeing "Press" stamped on his bench.

We were facing a judge. My first time. I was shaking by now. It was so overwhelming. The charges were read out. The lawyer was doing his bit for us. My legs were shaking and every regret was running through my mind.

Henny got a four-year driving ban and a heavy fine. Rusty got three months back in the nick. I was waiting... I got a three-year driving ban and a J95 fine. That was a lot in 1973, but at least I was out...

CHAPTER TWENTY

I got out of court. It was a nice December day. I only had a few bits of change in my pocket that I had when I got sent to the nick. Nobody was there to meet me at court, so I said goodbye to Henny and got the bus from town to Barlanark. I hated the place so much I wished I was back in the nick.

I got to the house: a second floor flat with a balcony. Shit hole. My ex-bird was there. *Why is she here?* I thought.

My ma gave me a hug. First in a long time. But I could see she was happy I got out. Turned out, when I got put in the nick, my ma and Skiddy Pants went to my ex-bird's parents' house and asked her to come back with me as I was getting into too much trouble. She agreed. Fuck, I didn't want this. Then to top it off, she handed me a present. I was embarrassed, but I didn't know she was gonny be there.

I opened it and what? It was a shirt, the same pattern and colour I wore in the nick. God's sake.

"Is this a joke?" I said, "Do I have another present in the cupboard?"

Then she said, "Well, I wasn't there to see you."

Okay, you win. Why does life have to be so complicated?

I was nearing the end of this part of my journey through the fields of complications. I managed to get my job back as an apprentice. I went back to day release college, got stuck in to the factory maintenance with Wattie the drunk and less on the mechanics. Old Alec was getting too grumpy.

We were lying under a van doing a gearbox and I fell asleep while waiting to hand him tools. He went mental with me, jumped up and banged his head. A sore one. Gave his head a bad cut. Then a week later, he asked me to jack up a van. He went under it before checking and the van came down on him. He was screaming and his wee legs were kicking like he was running lying down. We all got the van off of him and he was okay. A shoulder injury. But that was the end of him working. He was ready to retire.

He tried to blame me for the jack not being rightly in place. He made three major errors: never lie under a vehicle without axle stands, never blame an apprentice for your errors and never fall out with your apprentice.

Things were a lot happier without old grumpy Alec in the garage. Big Henny left also. His brother Rusty got thrown out of a top floor flat window at a party in Easterhouse and died. Henny took it bad.

I was getting on with things. Back with the ex to keep me out of trouble and I got a raise in my job. I wasn't getting chased in Barlanark at night, then at New Year, Ma was having a party. Skiddy Pants Jim wasn't there. She found out he'd been having an affair and all hell broke loose when he came home after midnight.

I jumped on his back as I thought he was going to hit my ma. My cousin Donald was in the house and he jumped on him too. Weird Da Jim ran out of the house with my ma going nuts. She sent us to look for him, but

I wasn't walking about Barlanark at that time at night. Too dangerous.

Next morning, I got up and things had calmed a bit. I looked out the window to see what the weather was like and the Cortina was up on bricks. Someone had nicked the chrome wheels. What next? I still had the old wheels in the cellar, so I put them on.

Then we found out Skiddy wasn't coming back. Ma went into depression and wouldn't work. Four kids below me. He'd fucked off again and I was left with the shit to deal with. We had no money, so I started stealing steak pies and stuff from work. I started stealing petrol from our pump and filling the van drivers' cars for half price. Again, all to feed the so-called family and also to pay my fine. I was heading from bad to worse again.

Then a summons arrived for the drink driving. I went to court and got a year ban and £50 fine on top of what I had already.

Two days after that, the bird told me she was pregnant.

"No, please, no," I screamed.

This was April '74.

I decided I had to get out of the madhouse and the life within it, kids I'd stolen to feed for, my ma crying every night drunk, a brother who, by this time, had major issues and fought with teachers then wouldn't go to school... I had to deal with that too. I'd had enough. Right, up to the council.

"I want a house," I said, "Kid on the way, baby due in January."

Skiddy must have heard about this and made an appearance and said I was mad to leave the house. Was I?

"This is your fine mess. You clean it up."

I got a house, got married in October '74 and baby was stillborn on his due arrival date, January 17th 1975. We named him Paul.

I went and got hitched for nothing. I had a wee house in which I did a lot of work myself and made a wee nursery all ready for baby. What now? Did I give it all up and go back to the madhouse in Apache territory? No chance.

I gave up my apprenticeship, again, and got a job sweeping the streets for a better wage. I hated the job and it was around the East End with a barrow, brush and shovel, hiding in case anyone I knew saw me.

I wrote to my old boss to get back into the garage. He took me back again, then boom, pregnant again. My beautiful daughter was born on November 27th 1975. I was nineteen. I was over the moon, but struggling again on a low wage and had to leave again.

I had a house, a daughter and debts…

I'm finishing this part of my journey now. I'm leaving with some thoughts. Do I have regrets? I have many. Too many to mention, but my story tells the sadness and reasons of my actions.

Did I learn anything? Yes, be wary of your friends and jealous negative people. If you're adopted into a family, you are not theirs, but I'll get into that another time.

What about school bullies? Teachers taught it by bullying weak pupils and getting away with it.

Any positives from life so far? Yes, always make sure your underwear is clean or it can affect the way your kids perceive you. It sticks with them, like his underpants stuck to him.

Smother your kids with good vibes and memories no matter what. Even if you're poor. It's not their fault. Don't argue or shout in front of them.

184

And love? The people who loved me left me in my younger years. I was left with the bad ones, but I love my kids more than anything, so I'm glad to say I've experienced that feeling.

Don't give your kids what you can't afford. It takes the fun out of it, but for God's sake give them something at Christmas. There's nothing less than nothing, but a little is better that nothing.

And finally, it's nice to be important, but it's more important to be nice.

Hopefully, I will be back with the later part of my life experiences. There are more to tell...

CHAPTER TWENTY-ONE

On January 15th, my son was born… I was delighted, but need to say I was surprised when the news of the pregnancy was given to me. I thought my missus was on prevention. Am I bad for saying that?

On my promotion and my short life of by now twenty-three and a half years, I was thinking back on my experiences so far. From fifteen years old, I'd had six jobs. Was this the big one? Had I hit the jackpot? I started thinking I could be a top manager by thirty, something never achieved in this company.

I had been told by Wullie that I was the youngest specialist in the history of the company. By now, the news was travelling down south where we had eight factories and the average age for a production specialist to start was about forty-five, and had to have a least ten to fifteen years' experience and to have been a supervisor first. Most of these guys where ex-army or navy and were engineers by trade. So, eyebrows were raised when my name and age was mentioned. And if they heard about my shift experiences with the women and the loonballs I mixed with to get where I was, they would have hit the streets to protest, I think.

My son was six weeks old and I was summoned up to Big Gerry's office. I hadn't been long in the job, but he was getting daily reports of my progress by my mentors. And I was attending the 10 a.m. meetings, so he was also watching my responses to what was being brought up. I wasn't afraid to speak out if I detected an injustice against the shift guys who got blamed for stuff they didn't do. Even though I guessed they did do it…

After the 10 a.m. meeting, he said to me to stay on. Also, Wullie and Big Jim were there. I thought, *Fuck, I've had it.*

His wee blonde PR girl by now was looking at me secretly with a soft grin on her face. I thought, *Well, I haven't touched her, so it can't be that.* Maybe he could read minds. If he could, I was really fucked as I was having some real dirty thoughts about this chick at meetings. If Big Gerry was doing her, it was curtains for me. So, I sat and waited for the tea woman to pour two cuppas all round and beat it out of the big oak double soundproofed doors.

I was sitting, waiting on the Gerry roar. He quietly spoke to us all.

"Right, everyone, I want your full attention. We have a problem down south with a production issue and the customer isn't happy. They need help and I've got the right person for the job."

I was thinking, *Shit, they're going to send Big Jim down and leave me to run the two shops. Please no. These fuckers will eat me alive.*

He said, "I'm sending young James down to sort it."

I still wasn't taking it all in as I was still in "Big Jim is going" mode. Nope, it was me.

Now my eyes were off the PR and locked onto Gerry, Jim and Wullie who were all grinning menacingly at me. They all knew. In fact, I later learnt it was Big Jim who was asked to go and it was he who said I was worthy of the job and that I should go down there and show them I was no mug. I was gob smacked. Speechless. Which was rare for me. Remember, I was almost twenty-four but built like a starving dog. Fit and fearless as I was, I was going into the lion's den and the only weapon I had was my tongue and cheek. And lions don't bargain with anyone. But it was now a done deal. I was going. Again, it was all back patting and well done. I was trying not to shit my overalls on the spot in front of the PR who was now giving me heavy stares. And I knew the look. I'd had it before from the kinky grave worshipper...

Big Gerry turned to the PR and said to her, "Annie, will you look after young James?"

He always called me that. Total respect for the guy. I guessed it was to differentiate the two Jims. I never asked why. I've been called worse.

She just smiled and said, "Leave it to me, sir. Will it be a flight?"

He said, "Yes."

My ears popped up. *Flight?* I thought. *Fuck me.*

"I've never flown, Gerry."

He laughed and said, "Well, you will be soon, son. You go down on Monday morning."

This was the Thursday. I was in heaven, thinking, *This is it. I'm now on the big platform.* I remember thinking in a minute about all the shit I had been through. The poverty, the schools, the beatings and that wee bastard Dada at school making me smell his stinking under arms while he had me in a headlock in front of the class and saying I was hopeless. And now I was sitting in a boardroom at twenty-four being sent to London on a flight to solve a problem for my company. *Wow, that's progress*, I thought. *I wish I could be in a class with you now, you wee pervert.*

On the Friday afternoon, I got a call to go see Annie the PR. I was nervous as I'd never spoken to her, but I'd been practising reading her mind. And her statistics. She had a shape on her, and a wedding ring... But, let's do one day at a time... Lovely song...

I went up to Gerry's office, but he was away for the day. So, it was me and her. I was filthy as we had a job on just started up, so I had been dripping in sweat. No flies this time. Just me and her.

"Come in, James," she said.

I said, "Look, Annie. I don't mind if you call me Jim."

She said, "Okay. I won't get you mixed up with the other one as I don't like him, so I don't speak to him much. But keep that between us."

Now I was in there thinking, *Sharing secrets already?*

She started giving me details of the flight and hotel, and a car would pick me up from my house to take me to Glasgow Airport. A car would also meet me at Heathrow and take me to the hotel in London, then take me to the factory. In other words, the car and driver were mine for the duration of the three days I was going to be there. I could not believe what I was hearing. What I could believe was she had opened another button on her already open blouse and I could smell her scent. And she knew it.

I stood up and she stood up. She was slightly smaller than me. I looked at her and thanked her for looking after me and gave her the stare. She just smiled and wished me luck.

I asked, "Will I need it?"

She said, "Yes, you will. They are a shower of ignorant bastards. I've met some of them."

I almost fell on my arse. I never imagined her swearing. She was a few years older than me, but well kept as we say up here.

CHAPTER TWENTY-TWO

Monday arrived. It was arranged for me to get picked up at my house about 6 a.m. I'd been lying awake all night for various reasons. Number one: I'd been thinking about my departure from Annie the blonde PR, the look in her eyes and what was under the sexy slightly unbuttoned blouse.

Number two: I'd never flown before and never had my own chauffeur before. Did I tip him and if so, how much? Major exciting this was.

Number three: what was I heading into when I got there? Who was I going to be advising and I knew I would get a difficult time. One thing worse than a Scotsman having to head down south to show them how it's done is a twenty-four-year-old Scotsman with a bit of a swagger doing it.

Number four: would I be able to fix the problem? If I did, I was going to make a few experienced older guys look very silly and I was going to be set for life in this company, and carry good street cred. And if I didn't, I was fucked for ever and the blonde would be wearing a polo neck.

I was en route to Glasgow Airport and adrenaline was pumping. I was like a kid going on my first holiday. Back then, you could get dropped off outside the airport entrance. I felt like Lord Muck, which in general means... usually derogatory... a poor person treated like an aristocrat for a short term. At that moment, I never gave a shit. I felt great. I gave the chauffeur a one pound note. He just looked at me.

I said, "Be on time for my return." He was fifteen minutes late for this one. "I'll give you another one pound."

I bet he couldn't sleep for the excitement for the next four days.

I arrived at Gatwick and by now I was getting tired and trying to find my way around was making me more tired. Then I saw a guy with a piece of cardboard with my surname on it. I thought, *Is he trying to show someone that this is his surname or is he looking for me?* Well, I'd never been in an airport, had I?

I went for the later. This guy was a chatterbox all the way to the hotel. It looked really nice, with a guy outside doing the door thing and all that. I was wise enough to know it was all for a tip, so I gave him a good tip: "In future, mate, bow when I come in and out and you will earn one pound."

The driver said he would pick me up at noon to take me to the factory. It was about 10 a.m. by this time, so I got to my room, lay on the bed and crashed out.

I was suddenly woken up by banging on the door. It was the hotel room guy to awaken me. My car had been waiting for twenty minutes for me. I jumped up. No shower, no change of clothes and starving.

Going back to my departure from the little sexy blonde... After she gave me the what's what about where I was heading, we got a bit close towards each other.

She whispered into my ear, in the sexiest softest little voice, "Good luck, you're going to need it, Jim, but I'll be here for you on your return."

That's why I couldn't fucking sleep. I could hear her, I could smell her, and, by now, could see what was under that blouse, and I was delirious. And to top it all, she

195

kissed me on the cheek. I was melting. Wedding ring or not, I was going to have her.

The journey to the factory was about thirty minutes. I remember the wheel man was yapping away. He apparently was from the East End, London. Well, I know the English always slag off the way we Scots speak and how they can't understand us. Go talk to an Eastender down there. I did not have a clue what he was saying and, to be honest, I don't think he did either. He was thick as shit.

We were about ten minutes away. I knew this as I could see the very large chimneys in the distance and the massive silos. All glass factories looked the same.

We rolled up to the front and I looked like shit. But hey, I wasn't here for a modelling job. I went in. Driver was to pick me up at 5:30 p.m.

I was met by an older woman who pretended she didn't know who I was or what my arrival was about. A tactic to unshelve me. Anyway, I gave her my name and who I was to meet.

About twenty minutes later, this older guy appeared. When I say older, to me he looked sixty plus, but he was in his forties. He was Bob. I later learnt that guys from

England who travel around the country, maybe sales guys or experts of some kind, are always called Bob or Brian, are fat and wear spectacles.

"Hello, you must be Jim, our saviour," he said with a silly grin

I retorted back, with a grin, "Well, Bobby, if you didn't require my expertise, I wouldn't be flown down here."

Now the grin had gone. It was only one way for me now and that was upwards as Bob and the ugly woman were pissed off.

"Come through for a coffee and we can discuss the main problem, Jim."

"Sorry, Bobby, it's tea for me."

I knew he wasn't liking the Bobby thing, but fuck him. He was christened now and it was staying. He started calling me Jimmy. Well, I was right at home now as we were all called Jimmy back home, but they didn't know that down here…

I got ushered to an office within the production end. Five guys of various ages, all above my age bar one guy who was only slightly older than me. Four had brown overall coats on and were clean. Well, that was a bad sign. That meant they were lazy fuckers and wanted to be gaffers. The younger guy had blue overalls on, but was clean also. I was introduced.

"This is Jimmy from Scotland who has come down to lend a hand. This is Paul… this is Brian…"

And the other three I can't remember who the fuck they were as I stopped at Brian to have a laugh.

So, I corrected Bobby. "Sorry, Bobby and Brian, but I'm not here to sweep up and lend a hand. I'm here to try and sort a problem that nobody here can fix, so I've been summoned by Big Gerry the Scottish manager to sort it."

Silence.

I was gaining points and enemies at the same time here.

"So, let's talk about where it's all going wrong and why I've been sent down."

They didn't know where to look. I was shitting it inside. I had a lot to lose here if I messed this up, but again I was showing no fear to these pricks who I knew by now had a game plan to screw me. Like the jokers from *The Hills Have Eyes* bin men in the shower room. If they never screwed me, then these jokers wouldn't. Been there, guys.

Bobby seemed to be the alpha male. Everything went through him. He was the advisor and the guy who never seemed to do any graft. Nobody appeared to disagree or argue with him, so I was going for him. Break the backbone, so to speak. I knew he couldn't fix the problem as he was the last stop, or so he would like to think. Next day for that one.

After about an hour of talking to them about the problem, it was decided I would go for the day back to my hotel.

I gave him a piece of paper and said, "Can you call this number? It's my car to take me to the hotel please."

The looks on their faces were something I will never forget.

"Err, right… okay… your car?" he asked.

"Yes, I have the use of a chauffeur-driven car for my duration here." And I just sat down.

Utter silence.

"One of us could have dropped you there."

I looked at him and said, "Why, Bobby, when I have the full use of the car?"

Big Gerry arranged all this. Now they all were twitching. Hilarious.

Next morning, I was up and ready for the day ahead. Now that I'd broken the ice, I wasn't worried at all. I knew I was dealing with lazy idiots and that was the biggest part of the problem they were having.

My man arrived on time and off we went. I'd got my overalls and kit with me. No brown coat as I was a grafter.

We arrived at the front reception and the woman said, "Just take a seat and I'll get Bob."

"It's okay," I said, "Bobby knows I'm coming. I shall head straight in."

I left her standing mouth wide open.

I made my way into the factory and into Bobby's office where he was reading a newspaper.

"Hi. I want to get started. What's the latest report on this production you're having issues with?"

He looked at Brian. "Oh, we haven't started on the plant yet."

"What?" I asked, "Why not? You need this job up and running ASAP as far as I'm aware. I was informed the client has been screaming at the managers about this. Where is your factory manager?"

"He's on holiday."

"Okay," I said, "Let's get in there and we will get an update from quality control."

So, off we went and without going into all the jargon, I got my kit out to take temperatures and stuff. Brian got sent to get me the production reports from the last twelve hours.

The problem they had was the shoulders of the finished bottles were thin and getting rejected by the hundreds by quality control. This lot had been given a week to find a solution, but couldn't find it. I read the report, pulled some samples off of the production belt and broke them up. I could see the problem, now I needed to find the cause. And I was also thinking every hour about Annie the sexy PR back in Glasgow.

I spent most of the day trying different situations. The machines had six sections all working in tandem. I would shut one off and use that as my test section.

201

About 5 p.m. that day, I'd made progress and I thought I knew the problem, so I called in the band of merry men to the office. I told them to shut down the whole machine at 7 a.m. the next morning, my last day, and I would be in about 7:30 a.m.

They asked what I was going to do and what my findings were.

No chance. These fuckers would sabotage my plans.

I said, "All will be revealed tomorrow. I have to phone Glasgow and get permission to do what I have to do." This was crap as Gerry told me to do what I had to do and he would back it, providing it was genuine and sensible.

Next morning, I was up and my driver was there at 7 a.m. for me outside. We arrived and I just went straight in, got ready and into the factory. I checked the machine which had stopped production. I started to set up my planned alteration and get it all made up. I got the line foreman to assist me in getting it fitted. It was a difficult job as we were two feet from the trickle of molten glass and the sweat runs off you, but I'd done this many times. You learn to overcome the extreme heat and burning pains.

I looked down to the shop floor and saw Bob and Brian and the others all staring up at me and the foreman. It was a very noisy area with the other three big machines all hammering out molten glass bottles. I could see they were all in confab, but I wasn't interested.

So, we headed down.

"Right, let's get this production going," I said to Ron the foreman. He was a good guy and knowledgeable.

Once in operation, it could take two to three hours to really start producing good glass, so it was time for me to get breakfast and dream about Annie for a couple of hours. Bobby instructed Ron to keep watch of the machine with the operator and pointed towards the door to me and off we went to the office.

"I'm sorry we weren't here for you, Jimmy. We start at 8."

I said, "In Glasgow, Bobby, we would be in the factory all night until we got this right. But then maybe that's why I'm here and you're not in Glasgow."

I gave a sly grin. I was loving this as I knew I was nearly at the end of this. My flight was at 7 p.m. at Gatwick, so I wanted out of here ASAP.

Bobby said, "Let's head up to the staff canteen and get breakfast."

"Great idea," I said, "I'm starving." As unlike them, I'd been grafting.

On arrival at the canteen, everyone knew Bobby. He was the Messiah, the village elder. But they were all curious as to who I was.

Breakfast was served. It was amazing and on the house. Five of us were sat around the table and the discussion started.

"Okay, Jimmy, what have you done so far and what do you think the outcome will be?"

"Patience," I said to them, "Let's see how this production comes out. Actually, I'm heading in now to start checking."

"Have another tea."

"No, I'm good, thanks."

I only had Annie and Big Gerry on my mind right now and I had to leave both of them with a big smile on their faces.

I headed onto the shop floor and I could see it was all up and running. Good. Ron informed me there had been no problems, but hadn't heard from quality control yet.

"Give it thirty minutes and we shall walk through to them and see what's going on."

Ten minutes later, the mob arrived on the shop floor and I knew they were wishing me the very best of bad luck on this. And I was nervous by now.

We all headed to quality control.

The boss said, "We're just testing the first complete batch of samples fit enough to be tested."

Now the bold Bob was holding court and taking over the conversation to the quality control boss, another Brian, but he seemed an okay guy.

I said to him, "Look, Brian, we will head back to production as this is going to take a bit of time. I'll be back in twenty minutes and can you keep your findings to me? If you don't mind. I've made several changes to

205

this production model and it's important nobody gets involved in changes at this stage."

"No problem, Jimmy, nobody but yourself first."

I looked at the mob and said, "No disrespect, lads, but this is my project."

Not a word from any of them.

We all headed back to production to monitor the machines.

After a while, I said to Bob, "I'm away to the toilet."

And off I went, but I made a diversion to quality control and headed for Brian the boss.

"Success, Jimmy! This is the first batch to pass everything. Keep them coming."

"Brilliant," I said, "We will do another test in thirty minutes, but we're sure it'll be good."

I headed back to the shop floor and the mob were still there. I got hold of Ron and told him the result, but to keep it from them for now.

We all headed to QC to see how the tests were. Again, success.

Brian said, "Think you've cracked it, Jimmy, by whatever changes you have made."

Yes! I thought.

It was now lunch time.

"Not for me, lads. I'm back to the hotel then airport."

"What about the production?" they asked.

"It's all good. Keep the production going as it is. I will monitor from Glasgow and also do a full report. Where's my car?" And that was it. No more problems on that line.

I arrived at the airport, gave the driver a five pound note (this was 1980, remember) and thanked him for his service and headed for the airport bar.

It was now after 5 p.m., so I decided not to call Big Gerry the manager or anyone else till I went in the next morning. So, I sat with my pint and wrote all my report out, including the new alterations I made, and like me, it was a work in progress. Couldn't wait to see Annie. And my two kids. Yes, it sounds very bad, but I'm being honest.

Next morning, I arrived at work. I went in a bit late and went to reception and saw Annie, looking sexy and smelling like a new rose, expecting her to ask how I had done down south.

She just said, "He's in, go right up. A few of them are having a meeting." She gave me that look and softly said, "I'll see you later, Jim."

I knocked on the big walnut door.

"Come in," I heard, very loudly from Big Gerry's loud rough tones. "Well, here he is, the United Glass Troubleshooter."

They all clapped hands.

"Well done, Jimmy lad," he said.

The door knocked and it was the tea lady with a big platter of breakfast rolls and pots of coffee and tea.

"Sit down. Wullie is on his way in. He doesn't know yet."

I was still a bit puzzled as I hadn't told them how I did or how the job had been running over night down south.

"Just to let you know, I've been tracking that job via the factory manager down there and this morning it's running at ninety-eight percent. You have done a magic number on it. Now tell us when Wullie arrives what you've done."

I said, "I've written a full report on it."

"Okay, Wullie will deal with that. Have your breakfast, then we all want to hear the full story. And I'm sure Bob Wilson will be your best fan," he said.

I knew he was being sarcastic.

Another knock at the door and it was Wullie, always a cigarette in his hand and always very smart in collar and tie.

"Good morning, gaffer," Gerry shouted, "Sit down and get a coffee and a roll. Young James has a story to tell us all."

Wullie looked at me. "Well, did you crack it?"

I just nodded positively.

"See, Gerry, I bloody told you."

At this point, the other Jim, who recommended me, said, "Hey, wait a minute, it was my deal. I put Jim forward for it. He's my success."

And they all laughed.

So, I sat and told them the whole story. The reception I got, how I fought my corner with wit and cheek and how I thought someone needed to look at the set-up there. I told them of my trials and failures and more trials, then success.

209

Gerry butted in and said to Wullie, "Jim has got a full report for you. When you read it, I want you to get on to their factory manager and ask why a raw twenty-five-year-old can do what four guys with a hundred years' service between them and good salaries could not do. Can you do that today, Wullie?"

"Gladly, Gerry." And he just smiled.

Big Gerry stood up with coffee in hand and said, "Let's toast young James on his successful mission and doing Glasgow proud."

They all stood up and toasted me. I was in awe. I couldn't believe what I was seeing and hearing.

He went on. "Since it's Friday, I'm taking us all out for a few pints tonight and a meal to celebrate. On the company. So, make sure you all order good beer and food."

He then called down for Annie to come to his office. My heart was beating.

He then said, "Right, Jim. Go with Wullie. Sit down with him and talk through everything. Make sure it's all on file as this could be a lesson to all factories."

We had nine all over the UK and two in Germany and Sweden.

Just at that, Annie appeared.

"Ah, my other saviour."

She just smiled.

"Right, Annie. Book a table for eight for tonight at an Italian restaurant in the East End. No, make it nine. There's a place for you. Can you make it, Annie?"

"Yes, Gerry, I can."

"Jim, after you finish with Wullie, go home and see your family. It's all good on the shop floor and we need you back fresh on Monday. But we'll see you tonight. Get a taxi and hand in expenses to Annie for everything, including what you spent down south, on Monday when you return to work."

Fuck, I thought. *She's going to see my tip to the mad chauffeur of £1… Okay, forget about claiming that one.*

I got home early, tired and wanting to spend time with my two kids. I had a two-hour sleep that afternoon, then got up all excited thinking about the night ahead, and what lay ahead.

We all met in a nice wine bar outside the East End. It was very posh. I had never been there before. Well, why would I have been there? Within twenty minutes or so, we were all there, except Annie…

I was having a pint of posh lager and wondering where she was. Big Gerry said we should give it fifteen minutes before we ordered. No mobile phones then, so waiting on people was the norm.

Just then, the door opened and in she came. She looked like a movie star. Not dressed to expose, but dressed to impress. And she sure impressed me. I could smell her scent as she approached us.

She sat opposite me, but next to Gerry. He made that clear by pointing to where she was to sit. I think there were two genuine reasons for this. First, he would want to talk shop to her as he lived and breathed work and she was his PA. Second, he knew a couple of the older managers there would be sniffing at her once they downed a few glasses of Dutch courage, as we all do.

We had a beautiful meal and once it was over, the big man wanted to say a few words to everyone. He loved doing this. If it was good words.

This was when he said to me, "Jim lad, come over here and sit next to me."

Oh oh, what was coming now?

He stood up and started giving them all the lowdown on my adventure down south and what it meant for the Scottish crew and all that stuff. During this, my head was pointed downwards as I was smelling Annie's seductive perfume and it was driving me mad. Just at that, she passed a piece of paper under my left thigh. My first thought was she was going to have a go at me under the table. Surely not…

I waited till Gerry was done and skipped into the toilet. On the note, it read: Here is my home phone number and my address. Call me about 10:45 tonight.

BOOM! Fireworks were going off in my whole body. I almost peed myself.

Back then, phone boxes were at every corner. Trouble was a lot of them were always vandalised.

Everyone retired about 10 p.m. that night. We all wished each other a nice weekend and taxis were laid on for us all. It turned out her address was only ten minutes from the venue, so I told the taxi driver to drop me off at a bar near her address. I knew for sure there would be a working phone in the pub.

I phoned and she answered in her sweet low voice. She was very quiet.

"Do you want to come here?" she asked, trying not to sound too keen.

I said, "Yes, okay. Is it all okay? Husband, kids…"

"We don't have children and he's on night shift."

Now I was panting like a hungry lion.

I said, "Okay, how's ten to fifteen minutes? I'll call a taxi."

"Okay, but don't stop outside my house, get off before."

"Okay, I will."

I kind of knew the area, but not her street. I got off and walked a block. It was approaching 11 p.m. She was waiting and opened the door for me. Her living room was dimly lit and the fire was on. She looked beautiful in the darkness. Now her top was hanging very open.

"Would you like a glass of wine?"

"Yes," I said, but I knew I would not drink it.

Within ten minutes, I'd got her on the floor on her thick carpet. I need to say it was the most romantic experience I had ever had. She was a few years older than me, but she was slim and gorgeous, like the mad grave

214

dancer I had the night of the full moon. Only this time no snow was falling, there was no screaming and nobody walking by us as we were getting down to it. This was so romantic and warm and private.

I left about 2 a.m. We had another three meetings at her house in the coming weeks and I took her out for a drink once also, but she was getting very nervous about being caught. We agreed protecting her was paramount, so it stopped with us both on very good terms. I will never forget the experience as long as I live. She said the same, funnily enough. I really think I would have given up everything to be with her, but I never got the chance to make that move.

In the coming months, I got on with my job and getting better at it. Big angry Jim left the job leaving me in charge of the operation. I was making good money and still seeing Annie every morning as I was now heading my department's morning meetings. It was amazing how we could communicate without speaking and using our eyes.

215

I started easing off and spending time with my kids and my wife. I had now bought our first flat and things were okay.

In May of that year, Big Gerry asked me if I was up for a week in Germany to learn about a new production that was maybe looming. I jumped at it. Of course I was up for it. It was meant to be in August, then in July I was on holiday. Right out of the blue, an announcement came over the radio that said our factory was closing at the end of that year 1983.

Thinking it was a mistake, I called the office. Big Gerry was very down and said the company had made the decision. I could not believe it. We had 500 people depending on this factory, but no U-turn was to come. Decision was made. The end of an era…

We went on till December that year and the gates closed. I got a decent redundancy payment and six weeks' salary in lieu. In all, about J3,000. A good amount then. Not like now. They hardly pay us anything.

I now had a heavy mortgage as the interest rate was fifteen percent after four years of the Iron Lady Margaret Thatcher's Tory rule. She was destroying Britain along with her co-pilot former Hollywood so-called actor Ronald (empty head) Regan of the USA… What a time we were having as a country back then. It was awful…

CHAPTER TWENTY-THREE

In the following January, I got a call from one of my ex-colleagues on a job that was advertised for bottle work operatives for a project in Kuwait. I looked at it with interest. They were paying big money, tax free, so the word got about and five of us applied to it. Myself, my wee mate Logo who with myself got beat up in the pub, big stammering Joe Oliver, Big John: a quality control manager, and an engineer foreman called wee Tommy. This guy thought he was a cut above the rest of us, even though he was only five feet tall... We all knew each other from working in the factory albeit different areas of expertise.

We all got accepted. By this time, I was really good at my job and it would have been a shame to let my skills get wasted. I had two kids to feed and a wife of whom I still didn't like, but for now she was needed to look after my kids.

The job was we were to join a crew in Kuwait to open a brand-new factory on the Kuwait Gulf. Now this was a job working directly with furnaces and molten glass inside, while temperatures were fifty degrees and above outside, but the money was amazing.

So, the deal was this new factory would have all new high speed production machines, way above anything I had seen or worked on, but they were going to send us to France for ten weeks first to get trained up on similar machines. Then we would go to Kuwait. Our salaries would be sent into our British banks every month and we would have very generous expenses to live in the little town in France near where the factory was, Chalon-sur-Sa□ne in the Bourgogne region. This meant absolutely fuck all to any of us, except wee Tommy who thought he could speak French. Uno, two-o, three-o. That was his version of French. What an arse he was…

So, we got a call from London and were told all instructions would be sent out to us by courier. I could not believe my eyes. We had tickets to fly to London, fly to Paris (first class with British Airways), fly to Geneva (first class, but can't remember which airline. But who cares when it's first class?), then we'd go by bus over the Alps to our destination, and J250 to see us for any expenses in the airports. We'd all struck gold.

By this time, big stammering deaf Joe had no money. He was completely skint. So, me and Logo put together to get him a few new cheap clothes for travelling. Joe had not a clue about any clothes or sizes. He lived alone and smoked a hundred a day and drank fifty cups of tea a day, so that was what his money went on. And one meal a day: chips and eggs, every fucking day.

I said, "Joe, put all that behind you. We're in the big money now."

He never heard me. Even if he did hear me, he was that excited he wouldn't be able to answer me.

I gave Poe a call to let him know about us. By now, he was settling in with Jeanette resigned to the fact he would not be working again. They got a new council house further into the East End and seemed happy to be there.

"Who is all going?"

So, I told him.

"What? You're taking that mad fucker Oliver? He can't hear and he can't speak without pissing his trousers.

How's he going to deal with the French and the Arabs? How the fuck are they going to deal with him?"

We both laughed.

"Aw well, Jimmy, you've done well in this game. Keep it going. Make as much money as you can and come home with bags full of money. Then me and you will hit the town with your wallet."

Aye, that was Poe.

One week later, we were on the way. It all happened so fast. It was January 1984.

We all were nervous, away from everyone for almost three months in France, then two years in Kuwait if the training all went as planned. We were told we would get home twice in the year. We agreed with money in our heads and not thinking of our families or how our kids would cope without us.

I got Big Joe and Logo together with three days to go. Reality was kicking in. Mine and Logo's wives were not happy about it all now. I had two kids and he had three.

Big stammering Joe had one son, but he only saw him when he needed some money, which wasn't often as he had none to ever give him.

I said, "Right, lads. This is up to you two, but I know what I'm gonna do. We go to France for the three months, do the training, let them think we're up for it and when the three months are up, we fuck off back to the UK. We're all young enough to find jobs."

They both agreed, so the plan was on.

Then Logo came up with a belter. "I'm terrified of flying."

"What? You've signed up, mate. We can't get there without flying. Why didn't you say?" Then I looked at Joe. "What?"

I could see he was building up for something and he was nervous.

"What?" I asked again.

"I'm scared too, Jimmy."

I said, "Wait a minute. You told me you went to Australia a few years ago to see your sister."

"I did," he said, "After six attempts."

"Well, did you go by fucking bus or what?"

"No," he said, "I flew there."

"Well, if you've flown to Australia, mate, I think you've broke your flying virginity."

"It wasn't the flying. I enjoyed that."

"Well, come on, Joe, tell me please. I can't wait to hear this one."

"It's the landing I'm scared of."

"Well, look, Joe. This may sound strange, but you can't fly without landing. If the plane doesn't land, we're in the shit, and that's a reason to be scared. Landing is good. It means, in most cases, you've arrived at your intended destination safely."

I felt like I was part of the Three Stooges.

I said, "Well, it's up to you two what you do, but I'm going."

So, we all agreed to go.

Logo said, "It's okay. I'll just have a couple of drinks to relax me."

Knowing he only ever drank straight vodka, I thought this was going to be interesting. God knows what plan the Aussie flyer had in his head. I wasn't going to ask him.

It all took me back to the first flight I had to London that Big Gerry sent me on. I was very nervous, but excited. I had no fear at all.

Someone said to me, "If you see the cockpit staff running for the doors with parachutes on, that's the time to shit yourself..."

I could have told these two this, but it would not have helped at all.

I for one know what it's like to be really scared, like when I was trying to protect my brother and sister when a guy had his head at our window at 2 a.m. when I was alone with them. Or when I heard a noise in the hallway and the two kids were in the bedroom trying to keep warm and I had got a poker shouting, "Where are you? I have a poker in my hand." I was eleven years old and trembling with fear. And also when I was needing a shower in the bin men dressing room with *The Hills Have Eyes* crew all staring at me with bars of soap in their hands. Yes, I know fear all right.

The morning arrived. A taxi was waiting outside to get us to the airport and the tears started. My kids were bawling their eyes out, as my wife was and I was. It was horrible as they were hanging on to me not to go, but I had to go. It was too late now to cancel.

The night before, I had to go to my mum's to say goodbye to her. She was paralysed completely down the one side having had a massive stroke and was very, very emotional. I was not looking forward to it, but it had to be done.

I headed to Logo's house to pick him up. I had called ahead to let him know I was on the way to give him enough time for the goodbyes. He was about a fifteen-minute drive away.

I got there and saw a suitcase sitting outside his house entrance. So, I waited and waited. Then I asked the driver to toot the horn, and I waited.

I eventually said to the driver, "Wait here, mate, please. I need to go see what's up."

As I approached the entrance, I could hear screaming. *What's going on?* I thought, so I banged on the door and it opened. I was faced with Logo and his wife having a fist fight in the bedroom and the kids were in the hallway screaming.

"Hey, hey. What the hell is going on here?"

I pulled them apart. He was all scratched and badly bleeding and she had a mark around her neck. She was going berserk.

Anyway, I calmed things down, got the kids sorted and told him to wash his face down and her to see to the kids. I had to go see the taxi driver to hold on a bit. We still had to go pick the other nutcase up also.

When I got back in, it turned out she didn't want him to go as she could not cope with the three kids on her own. So, I sat her down and explained the whole situation we were in and that I had planned to fuck off from France back home with plenty money until we all found jobs again.

Well, this bloody idiot never told her of the plan. He said to her he may not be back for six to nine months, but she would constantly get enough money to keep them. I looked at him and asked him why didn't he tell her this. He just shook his head, then I realised he was pissed out of his head and had not slept all night.

227

She calmed down a bit and we left. It was very emotional.

Now I was wondering what stammering Joe had in store for us. He lived alone, so it couldn't be that bad. He never had a phone, so I gave him an estimated time for pick up, which by now we were about an hour late for.

We arrived at his house, but there was no use doing the horn as he wouldn't hear it. So, I went and rung the very loud doorbell.

In an instant, he opened the door. Now, he was a good-looking big guy, slim, six feet tall, going bald. Sean Connery lookalike he was. I was looking at him. I could smell the horrible frying of stale oil smell and I noticed he had one very red eye.

"For fuck's sake," I silently said to myself. I needed to ask what was going on. "Are you ready? We're running very late, and why do I smell frying, and what happened to your eye?"

Now I was waiting as I saw he was trying to get it out.

"I'm frying my eggs."

"Why?" I asked.

"Put them on a sandwich for the airport."

"And the eye?"

"The hot oil sparked on my face and burnt my eye."

Jesus, can it get any worse? I thought.

"Okay, Joe, here it is. We're late. You don't need to make sandwiches up, we have money now to buy what we want. Get a cold wet cloth on your eye and please get us the fuck out of here ASAP."

So, I went back to the taxi and apologised again to driver.

"He's coming down, mate, two minutes."

The driver just nodded.

I looked at Logo and he was fast asleep. Then I saw Joe walking down the path. He had a red polo neck jumper on, a second-hand sheepskin jacket he bought which was way too small for him, and this mad red eye. It made him look very scary. He was carrying a tiny wee case.

"Is that it?" I asked.

"Aye, that's all I need."

"But we're away for three months."

"That's okay. I don't need much."

Fuck it, who was I to argue… What would be the point with this pair from *Deliverance* the movie. All I needed was a banjo…

Now, at last, we were on our way to the airport. We had plenty of time even though we had been held up. I smelt a horrible smell. It was from Joe with his horrible cooking and it had clung to his very small sheepskin jacket he was trying to wear.

I said, "Have you got those eggs you fried in that case?"

"Aye," he said, "I wasn't wasting them."

Now what I forgot to mention was that he had an Alsatian dog, which he always kept in a poorly made kennel out his backyard.

"Have you got Keeba sorted okay?"

"Aye," he said.

After a bit of a pause, I asked what arrangement he had made. To let you know, he had a lovely couple who lived below him in a nice four in a block building. Very polite and had lovely gardens. They all knew Joe was a bit odd, so they put up with him, with caution. His garden was a shithouse and stood out, and the dog constantly barked, mainly because it was cold and hungry. His take on it was it was the best way to train it…

I again asked where the dog was as I never heard it barking when I was at the door. I assumed he'd made an arrangement as it all happened too fast to do much thinking.

"It's in the kennel."

"In what kennel?" I asked.

"Roon the back."

"What do you mean? You're away for three months and it's fucking winter."

"It's okay. Joseph is going to come down every day and look after it."

Joseph was the vanishing drug smoking son I mentioned earlier that he hardly saw.

"Joe, look, mate, it's nothing to do with me, but he doesn't come to see you unless he needs money. Are you sure he's going to come and see the dog unless the dog has money in the kennel? And why wasn't she barking when I was at the door?"

"Oh, I gave her a big bone to keep her going till Joseph gets down."

"Have you told the neighbours of this?"

"No, they don't need to know anything."

"Okay. Good enough," I said.

What am I in for here? I thought…

We arrived at Glasgow Airport. Four suitcases, one small case and two headcases to deal with. I got Logo and woke him up. He was out cold and his bald head was bleeding again with the scratches on him. We all got out of the taxi and I paid the driver. He then asked if we were all going on holiday.

"No, mate. We're going into the unknown to live with each other for three months."

"I pity you, mate," he said and laughed.

We got checked in and the two of them, as expected, got pulled with customs. Of course they would. One was pissed and bleeding, the other had a pure red eye and clothes on that were way too small for him and stinking of fried eggs.

I waited thirty or so minutes till they came through. Customs surprisingly let them through after checking their paperwork, and seeing we were first-class flyers (well, from London we were) I could only assume, or they just said fuck it, let London decide on them...

We got through towards duty free and Logo was headed for vodka.

"Why do you want that?"

He said, "For a drink before we get on the plane to let me sleep or I'm not flying."

I said, "Well, Logo, at this point I give up on you, mate. You either fly or you don't. I don't give a fuck. I'm so stressed out with the pair of you I'm sorry I agreed to this. And, by the way, we are flying first class, where you will get all the food and drink you want. For free."

"We do?" he asked.

"Yes," I said, "So, there's no need to get bladdered before you get on, and chances are you won't get on anyway but it's your shout. I know I will be on it, and so will he..." I looked round and Smelly had gone. Oh no, where the fuck had he gone to?

He came back with bars of chocolate and tobacco and cigarettes.

I said, "What are you doing?"

"I'm getting chocolate and tobacco for Joseph for looking after Keeba."

I said, "Joe, we're three months away. The chocolate will be out of date or eaten by us, and also, we'll come though duty free on our return. And I would wait to see if Keeba is alive on your return before you hand out doggie care awards to Joseph. And you can buy cigarettes very cheap in France."

"No, I like Embassy fags for the gift coupons."

Again, I gave up.

Logo had bought his vodka at duty free. Back then, you could drink it on the plane. Nobody cared.

We got our flight to Heathrow. Logo slept for the short one-hour flight as he was pissed. Smelly Joe just stared out of the window and I was just thinking of what was ahead of us. The other two just stayed away from us, sat at the back of the plane. Back then, you could smoke on a plane.

We arrived at Heathrow and now we had to find our next flight. Logo was staggering all over the place and Joe was looking his scary self. He decided he was going to ask someone where to go. *Now, this I have to witness*, I thought. He was over six feet tall, bald, wearing a red polo neck jumper that was too big and a brown sheepskin jack that was too small. He had a pure red eye, a long black moustache and a fucking stammer like you never experienced in your life. He was stone deaf in one ear and he stank of fried eggs and chips. No fancy deodorants to cover smells back then. To kill the stink, we would have needed to cover him in malt vinegar.

So, off he went. He stopped a woman who just shrugged him off right away. He then approached a man carrying a case. Now, remember he was deaf and he had been working for fifteen years in a very noisy environment.

He shouted very loudly, "Hey, J-J-Jimmy! Do you know where—"

That was all he got out before the man told him to fuck off in an East London accent. In Glasgow, for anyone ignorant to it, if you don't know a guy's name and you need to speak to him, we just call him Jimmy. But not when in London.

We found our flight and got boarding. Logo was now very, very nervous, visibly shaking. Part fear and part needing a vodka. Or ten…

We got on a British Airways plane. Beautiful it was. Right up the front we were ushered into first class. I was totally amazed. Even back then you knew this was different. I felt like a king. Four air hostesses were there for us. Think I counted about ten or so passengers, mainly business people… and us. But fuck it, all the same price, all the same fun, no matter who's in first class.

There were massive seats to sit on and space all around us.

"I'll have a double vodka please," said Logo.

"As soon as we take off, sir, and we are in the air."

"No, I need it now. I can't take off."

I whispered, "Hey, you nutter, you still have some in the bottle in your bag. Be discrete."

236

Soon as the ladies turned their backs, he had it scoffed, then he passed out.

The other half was quiet. He just looked out of the window. It was at that moment I remember I felt very sorry for him. He had nobody except me and a dead-beat son. And the dog.

Once up in the air, the party started. We had all the drinks available and we had a good whack at them. We were having a ball. Big Joe, or Ivan the Terrible we nick-named him, was loving it. The other two in the party, wee Tommy and John, sat together. They'd had a few also. This wee Tommy guy I never knew very well. I knew he fancied himself as some big guy. He was five feet tall, in his shoes. He was asking for malt whiskies.

Logo shouted to him, "Hey, Tam. You sure you should be drinking malt whisky at your size?"

He retorted, "Well, firstly, you need to know your whiskies and I know a lot about whisky. Second, if you're gonna drink malts, you need to be able to handle them. And I can handle them."

Point taken, Tam boy.

We arrived at Paris airport. It was getting dark and I remember thinking about my wife and my kids for a moment. It was the drink making me emotional, so I snapped out of it and just thought about the kids.

We now had to find our way around. We were all pissed. Logo was rocking. He didn't remember the flight or anything about it. Then we noticed wee Tommy was missing. We heard a commotion and there were concourse staff all shouting and waving arms. Wee Tam was bent over a seat spewing his guts up. What a state of repair he was in. He was wrecked.

Yes, Tam, you do know your stuff on malts.

We left his big pal to deal with him. Big Joe was now pissed and this I had never seen before as he wasn't a drinker. Well, he drank gallons of tea…

He saw a little lady pushing a sort of trolley and galloped towards her to ask for a pot of tea. Well, she started screaming and threw a teapot at him and shouted for the police. *Fuck, what now?* I thought.

Next thing, two cops were there in seconds pointing rifles at him.

I jumped in shouting, "No, no. Ok-ok…" No, I wasn't stammering, I was shouting Ecosse and showing them first-class tickets.

They then calmed a bit, but they were looking at Big Joe with a very strange look. He didn't show he was drunk, but he looked like a guy who was homeless in the middle of Paris airport holding a first-class ticket. So funny.

The five of us now had to find our way to the next terminal and try to sober up. Wee Tam was still semi-conscious, but not my problem. I had my pal Logo to sort out. He kept asking me where we were and where we were going. I just ignored him.

Ahead, I saw a very long escalator/walkway going uphill. First time I'd seen one of those. Our main bags were getting transferred to the plane, so thank God we didn't need to carry them. Joe had only the carrier bag with his chocolate and cigarettes. Logo had a duty-free bag but I didn't know what was in it…

We got onto the escalator. It was all going good and we were halfway up the thing when Logo realised he was heading for a flight and flipped out. He said he wasn't going on it and headed to run down the conveyor. He tumbled and fell and his bag burst open. I saw a bottle of whisky getting smashed and he was tumbling backwards, somersaulting down the escalator and taking people with him like skittles.

I managed to grab him and hold him, but he was flipping out and his forehead was cut. We got to the exit and the same two cops were waiting on us. They then escorted us to the departure lounge with the warning to flight staff not to give us any more alcohol. I honestly think if we did not have first-class tickets we would have got jailed and sent home.

We got on a second plane to Geneva. Again, in first class. It was busy with rich-looking people. By now, everyone knew about us. Well, how could they not? Logo knocked half of them over on the escalator.

We got to our seats and the supervisor told us no alcohol at all. Soft drinks only. I was choking for a beer and got a coke. We then all crashed out for almost the whole duration of the short flight.

We landed and made our way to luggage collection. It was very cold and we looked dead. We had no idea what to do next and got our gear and took a seat to collect ourselves.

In a short time, we saw two guys with a board that said "Glasgow Party". That was our cue… We got loaded onto a mini bus. The guys spoke no English and off we headed. It was thick snow and perishingly cold. It was about 2 a.m. and we had massive hangovers. It was no use asking the guys anything as they could not understand, so we all fell asleep.

I awoke with getting bumped all over the rear seat. You know when you have been drunk and get woken up and you're not in the best of moods? Logo woke up just then too and let out a scream.

"We're on a plane again," he shouted.

I looked out of the window and couldn't see any road, just a black hole. Turned out, we were going over the Alps and it was snowing like mad and we were at the very edge of the winding road. Bloody scary it was. I decided to get back to sleep believing the drivers would look after out.

It was arrival time at our selected hotels. It was us first. I told Logo as well. He put his jacket over his head to blank it all out. It was early January. We were all tired and hungry. The guys dropped us off. Me, Ivan the Terrible and trembling Logo chose the same hotel because it was cheaper and we wanted to save as much as we could. The other two took a more expensive hotel, as they would. It was only minutes away from us, but they had a reception. We didn't. Ours was a free for all as much as we all had our own key. Like a hostel but we had our own rooms and shower with a communal kitchen, so we could cook and eat together, and it had a seventeen-inch TV. It was clean and looked okay. And we had a maid service every day to give it a clean. Ideal for us.

We had no idea where we were, but we knew someone was coming to see us later that day, explain everything and hand out expenses money in French Francs as it was then. To bed then.

I got woken by a loud knock on the door. It was a few hours after we arrived and two guys introduced themselves, but didn't speak English very well, but they seemed very polite.

They asked if we could go to the kitchen/sitting area. I walked in and the other two were already there. Logo was still drunk. He'd been at it before he went for a sleep and he looked like crap. Big Joe (Ivan) was in his underpants and still had the polo neck on and the red eye. One of the guys just kept staring at him. Hilarious.

So, we had important papers to sign and stuff and also had to find out our arrangements for starting in the factory the next morning. The guys also had our expenses money in Francs, so we got paid 250 Francs each for one week of expenses. About J38, which was excellent as this was 1985, so it spread well. Our hotel bill came off of that too, which was cheap as chips. Still plenty left to spend. Our salary of around J600 was secure to go into our British bank account each month, which was tax free. Excellent money for our wives to deal with, and Joe's son to buy drugs.

In the morning, we got picked up by a car to go to the factory.

The car arrived on time and off we went. It looked like a small industrial town. Few bars, restaurants, shops… We get to this massive glass container factory, very dark and smoky-looking. We went in and got introduced to the training and production team. A couple of them spoke decent English.

So, mainly the first week was classroom stuff about what we were going to be doing in Kuwait. They produced contracts for us to sign, but I quickly noticed they were in French and refused to sign them. The deal was after ten weeks, we'd travel right to Kuwait from France. Well, we three knew that wasn't going to happen. We never told the other two as I didn't trust them.

While the guys were talking to us, I was watching Ivan the Terrible. He was just staring into the light. I knew he hadn't a clue what was being said, but I could fill him in. They were all fixed on him too. One of the guys actually asked if he was Russian…

I said, "No, it's just the way he looks."

Wait till they tried to get a conversation going with him. Couldn't wait for that one…

We finished for the day and I led the assault on them regarding the contracts and said we, as a group, were not going onto the factory floor until satisfactory English written contracts were put to us. And also, we wanted a clause that within the first ten weeks any party could terminate the contract without penalties if not satisfied. We also needed two weeks to return home to sort our families out before we went to Kuwait and travel tickets home and expenses for the return flights from UK to Kuwait. We left them to think about it…

The next day, the agent came in with new contracts in English and they had all the terms I asked for. *Brilliant*, I thought. *That's us sorted.* So, we signed them.

We decided we should go find a restaurant in town that night to celebrate the contracts. After getting a shower and a change of clothes, we found this nice place called The

Piranha. It was a French/Italian place run by a married couple. He was a fiery Italian and she was a very sexy French woman called Pakita. He cooked, she served, obviously. But his eyes were always on her and we were a sight for sore eyes coming from Ecosse. The word got out and everyone was very curious of us, especially Ivan, and the way we spoke. Wee Tommy the toff tried to convince us he spoke French, but he didn't.

Anyway, we got a table. Now, in France, at least back then and there, when you sat down in a nice place, they expected you to be seated for three to four hours. You had bread by the baskets, wine by the gallon and salads and all sorts before the main meal came. I could see this Pakita was giving me the eye and the smile. I had the experience to know when the mating call was out there. We were looking at the menu, which was in French, and we hadn't a clue. Nobody around us spoke English, including the couple who ran the place, so Pakita was trying to help by looking at menu pictures. She kept laughing with us, enough to catch hubby's eyes and ears.

Me and Logo wanted steaks. Easy. Big Joe wanted chips.

"What? What the fuck do you mean, chips? Get something else."

"Sausages and chips then."

Fuck it, she could deal with him.

The night was going great. People seemed very friendly. We found they didn't like the English at all, but us being Scottish, Ecosse, they loved us and drinks were flying over to us.

Eventually, the mains came and we were looking forward to it. It was so cheap also. I looked at wee Tam's plate and it looked horrible. I asked him what the fuck he had ordered.

He said, "Seafood paella."

I said, "What the hell is paella?" I had never heard of it. Thankfully.

He said, "You need to know what you're talking about when ordering this type of dish."

I whispered to Logo, "Where have we heard this before?"

But he could not remember being out of his mind on the plane.

I said, "In first class… when he was drinking all the malts?"

But it didn't register.

"So, Tommy, you must be an expert on this food."

"Yes," he said, "I had it a lot when in Spain." He was pushing his fork through it all wondering what to do with it.

Idiot. There were shells, eyes, heads, all sorts of tentacles hanging out of the rice. *Fuck that*, I thought.

"You not fancy a bit of the old steak, Tommy lad?"

"No. Fish is better for you."

By now, Logo had caught on and we were having a laugh.

So, it all went by. We settled the very cheap bill and left a nice tip for Pakita.

We then went for a walk and found a decent-looking pub. We wandered in and ordered some beers and a double vodka for Logo. And, of course, the bold Tommy wanted the wine list.

"Here we go," I said to Logo.

So, we were all having our drinks and by now, we were pissed with all the table wine we guzzled. Tommy pointed to the wine and the waiter brought it.

Big Joe said, "Hey, Tam, why you no get a beer same as us?"

"Because, Joe, we're in France and the locals appreciate us trying the national spirit."

I said, "Tommy, it's Ricard."

"Oh, yes, but I meant wine."

"Aye, right, Tommy."

So, we were chatting and looking around and it was relaxing. I was moving to the bar to order more beers and I heard a thump and a scream and there was wee Tommy lying on the floor spewing his whole insides up. It was everywhere.

I said, "Forget the beers, barman. We're out of here."

They picked up wee Tam and carried him out. We got barred. First fucking night in town and this nutter had got us barred from the first pub. I was sure some of the fish from his paella were alive as they were moving in his vomit.

Yes, Tommy, you do need to know what you are ordering... Idiot.

We headed home to our hotels. Big John had to carry Tam. He was steaming drunk.

I shouted to him, "Next time, try the steak, Tommy." Ha ha ha.

Next morning, the guys were there to pick us up, but we diverted back the way towards the other hotel. I didn't notice that Tommy wasn't in the van. Big John said they couldn't wake him, so he guessed they were going back to get him.

We waited about fifteen minutes and next thing, two guys were carrying him out of the hotel.

"Can't you cancel class today? Look at him, he's ill."

"No, no. He must make class. Too important to miss. He must get up."

So, he did and my God, what a shape he was in. Sick stains all over his clothes. I truly wish we had mobile phones back then. We could have got some cracking photos of him. Only because he thought he was above us. It didn't stop him bragging throughout our time there. Some people just don't learn.

The following Friday night, some of the French guys decided to take us out for dinner and drinks, and we went to The Piranha as this was becoming our local place to go. The food was superb and cheap. It was all going great, but one of the guys noticed I was getting attention from Pakita. Like getting extra on my plate and big smiles.

So, he whispered to me, "What's going on with her?"

I said, "I don't know."

He said, "Be careful. Her husband has a temper. He is not well liked in this town. People don't come here because of him."

Okay, point taken.

I noticed wee Tommy had just ordered a steak and chips, but he was trying to tell her he wanted it well done and, as usual, didn't have a clue.

One of the guys said, "Hey, Mr Tommy, you must say 'bien cuit'."

"Yes, I know," he said, "She isn't understanding me."

"He's full of bullshit," I said to the French guy.

251

He knew what I meant and laughed.

So, the night was coming to an end. The place was busy and husband was too pre-occupied to watch his wife. So, the French guy had a quick chat with her, then came to me.

"Mr Jimmy, she is in love with you."

I laughed.

He said, "No, she is really and she wants to meet you."

"What? Me? You're kidding."

Now, we were six weeks or so into this gig and my hormones were jumping, as they always are, but this was serious. Fuck it.

"Yes, set it up, but don't say to the rest of them."

Monday morning, we were in the factory doing our stuff on the machines and in the afternoon, we did classroom stuff. So, we went up to class later and he pulled me aside.

He said, "She wants to pick you up at your hotel tomorrow night at 7 p.m. It's her night off."

I said, "How does she know my hotel?"

He said, "I told her."

"What about her mad husband?"

"That will be your problem," he said and laughed. "Are you okay for it as I need to call her and confirm."

"Yes, go for it." I was like a bull in heat with all this steak I was eating. And six weeks of living like a monk.

We went to work on Tuesday and on my mind was my dangerous date with this gorgeous French woman who was a few years older than me. Maybe a bit more. But she was a beauty and had a shape to go with her looks.

I kept thinking what would she say to her crazy husband to get away. Well, she must have a good excuse, I guessed.

We finished and the lads were discussing trying another bar for a drink and something to eat for a change after getting showered and changed. On the previous Saturday, we had a market in town, so Big Joe bought a couple of jumpers and trousers, so he was excited about that. He looked like Big Hen from the Broons, who were a Glasgow family back in the fifties.

I said to Logo, "Look, mate, I've got a wee bit of naughty to look at tonight. I'm jumping ship. Make an excuse for me."

He nodded and said, "Okay." He knew me well and didn't need to ask questions.

At 6:45, I was nervous and ready to go. I looked out of the window as it was very dark and I saw car lights on. That was her, it had to be. I jumped down and saw a big dark-coloured Mercedes car. I could see her sitting in the driving seat, so I jumped in.

"Hello, Pakita."

"Jim, je t'aime."

What the fuck was this? I'd forgotten she couldn't speak a word of English.

"Oh, okay. Yeah, me too."

Again, no mobiles then to translate.

She stuck her hand on my knee,

"Hold on, are we going somewhere out of here?" I said in my best French hand movements.

Just at that second, I heard a weird noise behind me. I froze and thought, *Fuck, it's a set-up. Mad Gino is behind me.* I turned round with caution and there was a toddler in a baby seat in the back seat. I screamed and started pointing at the baby.

"What is this?"

She looked at me puzzled. "Mon enfant."

"Yeah, I fucking know that. What's he doing here? Is he the driver while we're in the back seat? I don't think so."

She started crying and talking French.

I could now see this was a woman desperate to get away from her marriage and I was the ticket. I wanted to tell her I was desperate to get out of mine too, but without extra baggage like a French woman with a child and a maniac husband.

"No, no, no. No enfant. Not good."

Again, she was rabbling on in French.

I said, "Look, I need to go. Sorry about this. Next time, rules are: no underwear on and no children with you. Then we talk."

I fucked off out of the car pronto. I could hear her shouting my name, but I never looked back and headed for the pub around the corner I knew of, making sure she wasn't on my tail. By mere chance, the lads were in that pub. It was the nearest to our hotel.

They said, "The food is basic in here. We're going to head up to The Piranha."

"Not for me, lads. I'm just going to go back to the hotel and have a few drinks in my room…"

Next day in work, I told Gi what happened.

He said, "I will call her later on the classroom phone."

Once we went up to the classroom, all the French guys were aware of what was going on. He called her and asked if she was okay to speak. She said yes, then he put her on speaker phone. In front of everyone there.

Shit, I thought. *This isn't good for me.* She was crying and all I understood was my name she kept shouting. He told me she wanted to come to the UK with me.

"Yeah, I already guessed that one," I said. "Tell her I'm not going back to the UK as I'm going straight to Kuwait for a year. That will get her off my case."

"Okay," Gi said. "Now she wants to go to Kuwait with you."

Fuckers were all laughing.

"No, she's not allowed. Sorry."

We continued to go to The Piranha for the odd meal, but found another place out of harm's way.

CHAPTER TWENTY-FOUR

We all got through our training in different ways. We were in week nine of the ten we were scheduled to be there for. The agent appeared with our tickets, which again were first class, but this time we were straight from Paris to London with an overnight hotel in London to enable us to go to the Kuwait embassy there and sign paperwork. We also had tickets to Kuwait after two weeks at home and mega expenses to cover everything. I mean, very generous expenses.

We were due to leave France on the Monday. We got our gear together and bolted after saying our goodbyes to the French crew. Train to Paris, train to the airport, plane to London and plane to Glasgow and home. We partied on that Paris to London plane again. This time it was celebration time.

We had a fortune in money and all these tickets and had to get our heads together, so once we had a couple of days home with family and made sure the salary was in our bank, we decided to go see a lawyer I knew in the East End.

He said to us, "It's okay, you have the clause in your contract to terminate. That is your saviour, so you must write to them giving notice. Do it today, date it and send it special delivery along with the forwarding tickets and papers."

"What about the money?" I asked.

"Keep it. You won't hear any more about it."

We nervously followed his advice and did all he advised and kept the money. Fabulous, that was us sorted.

Then Ivan the Terrible told us he had got into trouble and needed to go to speak to the police.

"Why?" I asked without thinking.

"Keeba."

"Jesus, I meant to ask you about her."

In a very nervous stammer, he said, "Neighbours phoned the police as she was barking all night, was starving and emaciated."

As expected, his idiot son never bothered with her, so the dog was in a police compound until his return and Joe was in serious trouble.

I went to the police with him due to his stammer and deafness. Turned out, he gave his son his bank book and, having the same name, he was lifting money out as fast as it was going in for drink and drugs. Back then, it was easy to do this, but this was no surprise to any of us. He was a good for nothing guy who only thought of himself.

So, Joe got charged with animal cruelty, got summoned to court, got fined J100 plus expenses for the police and vet and was told never to own a dog again. Now he had a criminal record. The son? He hung himself some years later.

I got on with life. I got another job with British Rail and worked hard.

This was the story of the first thirty years of my crazy life. There's so much more to tell in the next thirty. More serious heartbreak, shocks, laughs and characters.

People ask, "Would you change anything if you could?"

My reply is, "Would you?"

Printed in Great Britain
by Amazon

21397679R00154